the stranger
in your house

the stranger in your house

Gregory L. Jantz, PhD

with ann mcmurray

David C Cook®

transforming lives together

THE STRANGER IN YOUR HOUSE
Published by David C Cook
4050 Lee Vance View
Colorado Springs, CO 80918 U.S.A.

David C Cook Distribution Canada
55 Woodslee Avenue, Paris, Ontario, Canada N3L 3E5

David C Cook U.K., Kingsway Communications
Eastbourne, East Sussex BN23 6NT, England

David C Cook and the graphic circle C logo
are registered trademarks of Cook Communications Ministries.

The website addresses recommended throughout this book are offered as a
resource to you. These websites are not intended in any way to be or imply an
endorsement on the part of David C Cook, nor do we vouch for their content.

The names mentioned throughout this book have been changed for privacy purposes.

Unless otherwise noted, all Scripture quotations are taken from the Holy Bible,
New International Version®, NIV®. Copyright © 1973, 1978, 1984 by Biblica,
Inc™. Used by permission of Zondervan. All rights reserved worldwide. www.
zondervan.com. Scripture quotations marked KJV are taken from the King James
Version of the Bible. (Public Domain.) Scripture quotations marked NASB are taken
from the *New American Standard Bible,* © Copyright 1960, 1995 by The Lockman
Foundation. Used by permission. Scripture quotations marked MSG are taken
from *THE MESSAGE.* Copyright © by Eugene H. Peterson 1993, 1994, 1995,
1996, 2000, 2001, 2002. Used by permission of NavPress Publishing Group.

LCCN 2011934292
ISBN 978-1-4347-6622-9
eISBN 978-0-7814-0790-8

© 2011 Gregory L. Jantz

The Team: Gudmund Lee, Susan Tjaden, Amy Kiechlin Konyndyk,
Nick Lee, Caitlyn York, Karen Athen

Cover Design: Micah Kandros Design, Micah Kandros
Cover Image: iStockPhoto

Printed in the United States of America
First Edition 2011

1 2 3 4 5 6 7 8 9 10

073111

To all those who parent and love teens.
Your efforts are worth more than you know.

Contents

Introduction   9

1 Who Are You, and What Have You Done with My Child?   13

2 What's Going On with Your Teen?   23

3 Emotional Roller Coasters Aren't Very Fun   41

4 Shaky Connections   69

5 This Is Your Body on Adolescence   89

6 When There's More Along for the Ride   121

7 When the Ride Goes Off Track   147

8 When It's Time to Get Help   165

9 Crisis of Belief   193

10 Powerful Parenting   215

Notes   235

Books by Gregory L. Jantz, PhD   238

Additional Resources   239

Introduction

You're the parent of an adolescent; when did that happen? Wasn't it just yesterday she couldn't wait to get home from school to tell you all about her day? And just before that, weren't you watching his T-ball game on Saturday? And the week before, weren't you parading her around in that polka-dot umbrella stroller? And the month before, wasn't he safe and snug in his crib? What happened?

Life happened and growth happened, and now you're heading into one of the most challenging seasons of parenting. I think adolescent parenting can be like slogging through ankle-deep sand: You make progress, but you never seem to get as far as you think you should for all that effort. There are times it hardly seems worth it. Those are the times this book is meant to address, because no matter how hard the adolescent years are, your teenager is worth the slogging.

The end of your parenting may be visible on the distant horizon, but you're not done yet. No matter how loudly and passionately your teen tells you to keep out, you need to stay in; you need to stay involved and stay alert. You need to watch to see if your teen is exhibiting the natural angst of this age or if there's something more serious going on. This book will help you determine where that line is and what to do if that line is crossed. Some of the examples in the book may seem extreme, and you may have a "not my kid" reaction. If it's not your kid today, that's wonderful and a relief, but what about tomorrow or the day after? And however extreme an example may seem to you, these are real things that real kids are dealing with. If not your kid, then maybe someone he or she knows; if not today, then maybe tomorrow.

Just because you're tired of slogging through the sand, now's not the time to put your head in it. Sure, it would be easier in some ways to ignore those nagging feelings and just pretend they don't exist. But if your gut is telling you there's something wrong or just not quite right, even if you can't put your finger on it, trust that feeling enough to read this book. If you no longer recognize the teenager in your house as the same child you raised, or if you have an ongoing disconnect or worsening relationship with your teen, continue to read even if you wish this would all somehow just go away. There are reasons and answers and help if you'll just keep slogging. Some of the answers may require action on your part. Some of the answers may allow you to relax and realize your teen's life is just temporarily overwhelmed, not permanently undone. Knowledge is power—for you and your teen.

How to Use This Book

At the end of each chapter, I have included activities and self-evaluation questions in a section called "Bringing It Home." This is the part where you get to pour out your thoughts, your hopes, your desires, your fears. I encourage you to write down your answers (either in the book or in another notebook) after each chapter, before moving on to the next. Talk about your answers, as appropriate, with family and friends. Use them as a springboard to take the concepts and information presented in each chapter, and claim them individually for yourself and for your family. The Bringing It Home section is a way for you to become your own best source for understanding, clarity, and direction. I have found over the years that deep down most people know what they need to do; they just need to find the strength and purpose and way to do it.

After you've completed the whole book, go over each Bringing It Home section again. I can't help but feel you'll be surprised at what has stayed consistent and what has changed over the course of reading the book.

In the final analysis, yes, this is a book about your teenager, but it is also very much a book about you. The more you understand about your teenager and yourself, the closer together you can become.

As you read the pages that follow, I hope you have an open and transparent heart. This time of adolescence is not just a milestone for your teenager; it's also one for you. It is a time for you to learn, adapt, and grow as a parent and as a person. Maturity can happen at any age.

It's time to get to know that stranger in your house.

1

Who Are You, and What Have You Done with My Child?

He's in his room for what seems like days, emerging periodically and answering questions with sullen, monosyllabic responses.

She's moody, teary, and irritable, one minute demanding you drop everything to tend to her needs and the next minute demanding you just leave her alone!

He's not going out for tennis this year, even though he did well last year. When you ask him why, he can't really give you an answer, other than he's not interested anymore. As you think about it, there are a lot of things he just doesn't seem that interested in anymore. He seems to fill up his time somehow, but you're not sure with what. When he was younger, his life was an open book; now, he's closed the cover and locked you out.

She's constantly negative—about everything. Nothing ever goes right; she never looks right; you never act right. She used to be a fairly happy kid, but now she's just difficult to be around, which kind of works out because you hardly ever see her anyway.

He complains about headaches and not feeling well. It's hard to get him up in the morning to go to school. If he could sleep until noon every day, you think he would, and suspect he does when you need to leave early for work.

She's rarely at the dinner table anymore. Instead, she says she's already eaten, grabs a bag of chips and a soda, and goes to her room. When you ask her about it, she says she's too busy to spend time with the family and prefers to work in her room, but you're not exactly sure what she's doing in there.

He used to spend hours chattering away about all sorts of things; you used to spend time together. Now, having a root canal seems higher on his priority list than spending any time with you.

As sure as she is that she'd really rather not spend time with the family anymore, that seems to be all she's sure about. It takes her what seems like hours to get dressed in the morning, her chair piled high with discarded outfits. She doesn't know what she wants to do or what she wants to eat, and getting her to sit down to do her homework is almost unbearable.

You know he's got clean clothes because you do the laundry, but he seems to constantly wear the same clothes you could swear he went to bed in. His hair is never combed, and you're worried about how often he's doing things like brushing his teeth and wearing deodorant. He never seems to stand still long enough for you to really tell. Instead, you see more of his backside leaving than anything else about him.

You're living on pins and needles, wanting to maintain family rules and responsibilities for the sake of the younger kids, but it's sheer torture to get any sort of commitment from her to do her chores. She always promises to do them later, but, somehow, that later never seems to happen. It's often more tiring to keep asking her to do her chores, so you end up just doing them yourself.

Sunday mornings are even worse than weekday mornings. Getting him up and ready for church hardly seems worth it. He used to go willingly, but now there's always a reason why not. Just getting him in the car is a thirty-minute argument.

All of this wouldn't be so bad if you didn't get that sense in your gut that your teen is unhappy. It's as if he or she walks around in a swirling cloud of discontent, frustration, and irritation. Sometimes it's so thick you have trouble making out the person inside. It hurts because that person is still your child, no matter the age.

Rough Ride

Few things strike fear into the heart of parents more than the approaching adolescence of their children. They've heard horror stories from family and friends, and they dread the fear of the unknown and how it's going to go with their own kids. Will that happy-go-lucky child turn into some sort of a sullen monster? Will the childhood skirmishes of yesterday turn into open warfare? Will the days of having their friends over all the time turn into years of going out to be with friends somewhere else?

Most of us can remember feeling awkward, unattractive, anxious, and overwhelmed as teenagers. We remember living under our own swirling cloud of discontent, especially with our parents and with our own bodies. Sometimes it seemed like we lived in a box, with all four sides pressing inward, squeezing us. Other times, we just wanted to explode out of that box. For several years, our lives were a roller coaster: It was a wild ride, terrifying and exhilarating. As parents, it's not something we necessarily look forward to repeating with our own kids.

The roller coaster of adolescence is so prevalent, so stereotypical in some ways, it's developed into a sort of cultural shorthand. Just say the words *teen angst* to a group of parents of adolescents, and heads will nod. It's a universal catchphrase for anything from explosive anger to all-is-lost despair. Even kids who weather their teenage years with relative calm still undergo times of double loops with gut-wrenching climbs and terrifying falls because no one is totally immune to adolescence—or life, for that matter.

You knew this ride was coming. Most of you willingly got in line years ago, when you took that sweet, beautiful baby home from the hospital. It's been years in the making, but now you're once again in the midst of that tumultuous phase of life known as adolescence. But this time it's not you in the driver's seat; you're along for the ride, but how high you climb and how far you fall are no longer merely dependent upon you. Just when you thought you were supposed to be carefully "letting go," your child's behavior does nothing but make you want to hang on tighter—or sometimes it makes you seriously consider letting go altogether from sheer exasperation. It was hard enough, frankly, to survive your own teenage years; how are you supposed to help your child survive his or hers?

It's a weird time of life for a parent. You're still responsible for your teenager physically, morally, and certainly financially; but your teen is taking on, trying on, and experimenting with more and more of his or her own responsibility. How far should that experimentation go? How far is far enough, and when it is too far?

But what if your teen is experiencing more than just the normal ups and downs of adolescence? How can you tell? More than likely, all you've got to go on is what you experienced yourself as a teen, but is that really the baseline you should use with your own teen? What if there are fewer and fewer ups and more and more downs? Is your teenager in a "phase," or has that "phase" spiraled into something more serious? As a parent, you're expected to know the difference—without any training and while you're in the midst of the moment yourself. You're supposed to be able to diagnose a teenager who makes it his or her life mission to give you as little personal information as possible. This doesn't appear to be a recipe for success.

None of us want our kids to be miserable as they're transitioning from child to adult. And none of us, frankly, want to be miserable ourselves, weathering an incessant barrage of teenage moods and behaviors. Navigating this time of life can be complicated, and it's perfectly reasonable to reach out for some answers and some help. That's what this book is designed to do. It's written to provide you with information so you can better understand

- what your teenager's behavior means;
- when to relax and ride the wave of a teenage phase without pushing the panic button yourself;
- how teenagers get off track and how to help them get back on the right track;
- how to know if behavior reflects "just being a teen" or if it's something more serious like clinical depression;
- what behaviors you can work with and which ones you can't;
- how to help your teen understand the God-designed future and promise waiting at his or her cusp of adulthood;
- when it's time to get your teen professional help and how to choose the option best for your family and situation.

As a professional counselor for well over twenty-five years, I've devoted a good portion of my practice to working with teenagers. I've found them to be amazingly forthright and courageous, while at the same time vulnerable and confused. Often, they are doing what seems best to them to address their situation. Unfortunately, they often turn to risky and destructive behaviors as coping strategies through this turbulent time. When these coping behaviors end up taking on an ugly life of their own, the roller-coaster ride turns very dangerous. It doesn't have to be this way.

Teenagers are on the cusp of their future. They're still grounded in childhood but can easily see adulthood just off in the distance. They're chomping at the bit to grow up and dragging their feet at the same time. Teenagers are on a mission toward that adulthood in the distance; they just need help navigating the path. You can't take the steps for them, but you can help make the way clearer. It's important to their development that they navigate this journey well and on their own, supported by you.

Detours at this age have long-range consequences. Closing the bedroom door—either as the teen or as the parent—on the problem isn't going to make it go away. As a parent, you need to be ready to assist, even if your teen insists he or she absolutely does not want your help. This isn't meddling; it's parenting.

Because teenagers see themselves differently and consequently see parents differently, your commitment to your teen's future is more complicated. When he stubbed his toe on the sidewalk curb at four and a half, a kiss, a hug, and a cartoon Band-Aid did the trick. When he stubs his heart on his first romantic rejection, it's a little more complicated. When she refused to like the outfit you picked out for her at five, you had others to choose from. When she refuses to like herself at thirteen, it's a little more complicated. When it became a contest of wills with him at eight, you could win and still get a hug at the end of the evening. When it's a contest of wills at fifteen and there's no way he's prepared to give in to you at all, it's a little more complicated. When she was ten and you wanted to spend time together, there was nothing she wanted to do more. When she's sixteen and you want to spend time together and she just looks at you with shocked disbelief and adopts a when-hell-freezes-over expression, it's a little more complicated.

Each phase of life has its own challenges. Parenting has never been for the weak-stomached (especially during the early years), the fainthearted, or the halfway committed. It can be tempting to take a backseat when your kid hits the teen years, figuring you've done the bulk of your work and you can just coast into his or her adulthood on all your previous parenting momentum. You're older, more tired, and your less-than-active participation in their lives pretty much seems what teenagers want anyway. It's tempting, yes, but don't give in. You're still the parent; you're still the adult, and you still have work to do. Even if it doesn't seem that way, your teenager desperately longs to be connected to you. He or she needs (notice I didn't say *wants*) your acceptance, acknowledgment, and approval. No matter how much they argue to the contrary, teenagers—including yours—do not have life figured out yet. They don't need you to live their lives for them, but they do need your guidance and your support, even when that's the furthest thing from their minds and hearts.

And when that roller coaster goes off track, teenagers need some-one to notice and take immediate steps to get things on the right path. Partnering together with your teenager to successfully navigate adolescence is one of the hardest things you'll ever do. It also has the outrageous potential to be the most rewarding.

Bringing It Home

When you think about your child becoming or being a teenager, what three words or phrases come mostly quickly to mind?

1.

2.

3.

For each one, identify a specific incident or event that gives this feeling such validity in your mind. Please keep in mind that this could be something from your own adolescence that you're projecting onto your teenager.

If the attitude of parents of teenagers could be culled down to a single word, it could be *concerned*. Do any of the three words you've written above fall into a concerned or fear category? If they do, what are you concerned or fearful about?

In order to help remind you that all of this work and effort is worth it, I'd like you to create a photomontage of the teen in question, using at least five photographs of your child, ranging from infancy to the present. How you create the montage and where you put it is up to you, as long as it's easily accessible. Here are some ideas, or you can come up with your own: a framed collection on your nightstand, a rotating screen saver on your computer, downloads on your cell phone, or simply individual photos in your purse or wallet. How you access them isn't as important as looking at them regularly. You need to remember and remind yourself that all of this is worth it and that you love your adolescent, even when his or her behavior seems specifically designed to call that love into serious question.

2

What's Going On with Your Teen?

His door was shut, as usual. It was quiet, which wasn't unusual. If he was on the computer, she could hear it—but if he was listening to music, he'd have his earbuds in, and she couldn't. She wasn't sure which one made her feel better because frankly both frightened her a little. It had started as an uneasy feeling about three months earlier. Jake just wasn't acting normal—nothing Tanya could put her finger on, but things just didn't seem right. She'd been putting off really thinking about her worries since then, telling herself over and over again he was entering adolescence and that's just the way it was.

Walking past his room, down the hall to her own, Tanya sloughed off her shoes and dropped her purse on the dresser. It had been a long day at work, and she was glad to be home. She was looking forward to a quiet dinner and some time to relax. Julie was over at a friend's house and would be home in about thirty minutes, just long enough for Tanya to put something together and on the table. It had been a while since she'd made spaghetti. It was Jake's favorite; at least it used to be. She didn't know anymore; it seemed like so many things she thought she knew about him were changing.

She'd heard countless parents moan and joke, sometimes simultaneously, about losing their kids through these teen years. Stories of happy, contented children transforming into surly strangers, eventually emerging from emotional hibernation in their early twenties. Tanya didn't want to wait that long. She could feel Jake slipping into that pattern and had no idea what to do. Was it just a phase? Would he snap out of it? How quiet was too quiet? What did he do in his room for hours at a time? Why would he barely even talk to her anymore?

Tanya didn't want to pry and risk pushing him further away, but her sense of unease was growing. With Julie, she kind of knew what to expect; after all, Tanya had been a teenage girl herself once. With Jake, the whole gender thing came into play, and she felt adrift in strange waters. No kid wanted an overbearing mother interfering in his life— but were her concerns overbearing, or was she just being a worried mom? Tanya wanted to talk to him, to ask him what was going on, but she was afraid of his reaction, afraid of being rejected, so she walked down the hallway, past his room, without saying anything. Perhaps the smell of dinner would coax him out.

Dealing with children in general is not an easy job assignment. Each stage of development has its own challenges, and each parent comes equipped—or not—to handle those phases. Some parents have difficulty with the young infant stage, feeling totally overwhelmed by an inexplicably crying baby who's unable to articulate what's wrong and immune to any sort of verbal reasoning. Other parents cringe at the defiant toddler stage, where eternal vigilance is the price of parenting, as anything that can go wrong seems to with a curious, tottering child. There is something comforting, almost, when children get to school age; they are verbal and easier to figure out. They can be so sweet and endearing, wanting to be with you, and mostly malleable. Then adolescence hits, and all bets are off. What used to work doesn't anymore. Your relationship begins a quantum shift, in agonizing slow motion, excruciatingly drawn out over a period of years. Your kids hitting adolescence is like you hitting a brick wall going forty. At least, that's how the popular wisdom goes. Perhaps you can relate to one mom's observation: "All the early parenting books I read forewarned me of the 'terrible twos,' but nothing prepared me for the 'traumatic teens.'"

Whether or not you particularly remember your own adolescence (and many people try very, very hard not to, for a variety of reasons), there are just some universal characteristics that have become stereotypical for teenagers. The grumpiness, the irritability, the isolation, and the scattershot anger are part and parcel of the adolescent phase. The teen's desire to be with friends and definitely not to be with Mom or Dad can smack a parent full in the face with its sudden appearance, sometimes in the preteen years. Where you once were a source of knowledge and wisdom, now you're clueless and technologically inept. Where once your age gave you cache, now your age is merely aged. Easy kisses become stilted, embarrassing encounters, over promptly with a quick swipe to the mouth or face. Adolescence is the beginning of relationship alteration, an alienation with both sides firmly convinced of the alienness of the other.

Shedding Skin

I think the nearest comparison I could give to what I remember about being a teen and what I hear from teenagers about adolescence is that of a reptile shedding its skin. When a snake or a lizard sheds its skin, the new growing skin cells separate from the old established skin cells, causing a marked change in appearance and producing an irritability that can result in increased snapping and hissing. Of course, reptiles shed their skin relatively quickly, so the analogy doesn't carry too far. Still, I think it's fairly parallel. Your teenager's nascent adult is separating from the confinement of childhood, causing a marked change in appearance and producing an irritability that can result in increased snapping and hissing. I think it's why teens often feel like their skin is crawling and fight against a sensation of being confined, wanting to burst free. And it's why parents often look at their teens as though they're something that just crawled out from under a rock.

Shedding skin is uncomfortable, often disturbing, and absolutely necessary for growth—and it's the same with adolescence. It makes it easier, however, when you know what to look for and what it all means. Teenager adolescent behaviors are stereotypical for a reason—they are fairly consistent across generations. If you haven't noticed many of these already, you will, in varying degrees, depending upon your teen.

- *Moody and irritable*—Teens seem to combine the attention span of two-year-olds and the patience level of three-year-olds with the verbal acerbity of the harshest stand-up comic. The same remark from you delivered without incident eighty-three times can all of a sudden be met with a blast of condemnation and scorn on the eighty-fourth rendition.
- *Unpredictable*—Teens seem to vacillate between alternate dimensions. In one, they are competent, I-can-do-it-so-don't-help-me near-adults, and in the other they are why-haven't-you-helped-me-sooner

children wailing at the top of their lungs. They phase in and out of these dimensions at will, leaving you constantly on edge and wary of which persona you're going to encounter at any given time.

- *Manipulative*—Teens are trying out their ability to (a) use logic to get what they want; (b) use repetition to get what they want; (c) use persuasion to get what they want; and (d) use guilt to get what they want. They will try various methods to gain their ultimate objective—to get what they want. In some ways, they are like highly verbal, moderately sophisticated toddlers, with an eye firmly focused on that shiny toy or piece of candy. Their drive to yell, "Mine!" is as strong, if not more determined, as that toddler's; being older, they're just more inventive about finding the way to get it.

- *Argumentative*—Sometimes teens argue just for the sake of arguing. They know before they start that they're probably not going to get what they want, so they settle for second best—a good argument. This allows them to vent off steam, to transfer their own displeasure in life to you, and to test boundaries. In a strange way that you can probably understand, it feels good to your teen, or at least it feels better than being tied up in knots inside. You become a symbolic punching bag for your teen's emotional workout through argument and anger. Your relationship with your teen has been targeted for his or her own adolescent "challenge course," where every boundary that gets challenged is yours.

- *Withdrawn*—When teens withdraw, they usually are selective; they withdraw from you but not from their friends. Where you were once Plan A on their list of favorite things, you're now in the T and U category; in other words, way down the list … unless they want something, and then you're back to A status—but only until they've obtained whatever it is they want or have conceded temporary defeat.

- *Self-absorbed*—Teens think the world revolves around them; they are at the gravitational center of everything that happens to, in, and around them. The family, you, other people, other reasons are peripheral and, thus, not as important. To teens it really is all about them. There is no "the world"; there is only "their world," which is different from yours and which they are sure you couldn't possibly understand.

- *Dramatic*—During the teen years, the color gray ceases to exist. Instead, everything that happens is thrust into stark and dramatic black or white. Another way to put this is that the teen years are all about intensity. Feelings and emotions are magnified and modified, not unlike one of those fun-house mirrors where images are bent and warped out of all normal proportions. You look at what's happening and see one image, while your teen is experiencing that same image as something completely different. This is the teen world of extremes, and, as such, it's a much scarier world than yours.

- *Dismissive*—In order to disguise the intensity of emotions and feelings twisting around on the inside and outside, teens will often take a global *whatever* attitude. Barely entering adulthood, they already display a sort of world-weary, seen-it-all, bored demeanor, especially where you as a parent and your rules are concerned.

- *Collectively independent*—Teenagers tend to try on identities like outfits, looking for ones that seem to fit or look good to them. The goal appears to be establishing independence, but that independence is deceptive. Seeking *independence* from you is designed to produce *acceptance* from the collective group of peers. It's an odd dichotomy of seeking approval from one group by displaying disdain for approval from another.

- *Anxious*—Teenagers have a great deal to be anxious about because so much of their essential nature is changing. Their bodies are changing; their goals are changing; their anchor points in life are changing. It's as if the ground beneath them is shifting, and, at any given moment, they have trouble finding their bearings. As much as the idea of being independent and away from you is exhilarating, it's also terrifying. On this roller coaster, they are firmly at the front of the car, even when they'd like nothing more than to crawl into the seat behind you.

- *Powerful*—Of all the characteristics of teenagers, this can be one of the most disconcerting. Teenagers are moving from a reality where adults can usually be counted on to be more capable, more competent, and more able. This provides stability and security. They are moving to a reality where they may find themselves in the uncomfortable and often frightening position of power. Teens can be physically larger and stronger than the adults in their lives. In a technologically shifting world, they often find themselves more adept, more intuitive, and more savvy than many adults. Being in charge, as teens instinctively know, carries with it both a blessing and a curse. They are attracted to the power but intimidated by the responsibility that comes with it.

- *Exclusively inclusive*—Teens act naturally like pack animals, even when loudly proclaiming their fierce independence. Most teens crave a sense of belonging, even if they are unable to find it in the people around them. Because of the way culture has shifted, an inclusive community for teenagers doesn't necessarily need to contain the kids on the block or a group at school. There are online communities and affiliations based upon clothes, music, hairstyles, causes, disaffections, or just about anything else a teen wants to affiliate with. A band of brothers, sisters, or both is only a Google search away.

- *Physically awkward*—Teens are still in the process of growing into their bodies, which can put them at odds with that very same body. Physical sexual development can run ahead of a teen being emotionally and cognitively ready to handle those changes. This leaves teens often feeling distinctly out of phase with their morphing bodies and the resulting emotional fallout.

- *Overwhelmed*—Teenagers, as the saying goes, have eyes bigger than their stomachs about all sorts of things besides food. This tendency results in some kids with schedules so packed, it's dizzying. There are teens who seem to career from event to event, propelled by sheer forward momentum. This drive to do can be as much their need to avoid saying no as it is any real desire to say yes. These teens cheat themselves on the important in order to feed the urgent. Getting proper sleep on a nightly basis is exchanged for

over-hours-catch-up-whenever-possible on weekends and no-school days. Proper nutrition is
jettisoned for anything that is quick and convenient and packs a four-hour punch. They are
short tempered, stressed, and at their wits end,
all before school starts at seven fifteen in the
morning—and the day doesn't get any better
from there.

- *Insecure*—For all their protestations and loud
proclamations to the contrary, teens are simply
not as sure of themselves as they insist. Even
those who fall into the age-old categories of
most attractive, most athletic, most popular,
most humorous, most rebellious, or most avant-
garde live daily on the knife's edge of horrifying
humiliation. The distance from most to least is
agonizingly short, at least from a teen's vantage
point. Nothing is secure when every day is fraught
with worries, fears, and potential disasters waiting around the next corner, the next encounter,
the next relationship.

Empathy

We started out this chapter talking about how alien teenagers can
seem and how, frankly, unsympathetic you can feel toward your teen.
Hopefully, going over this list of teenage characteristics has reawak-
ened latent empathy for your kid. That latent empathy may have

come wrapped up in painful remembrances of being a teen yourself. It may even have spurred some of you to mutter, "Better her than me!" You know yourself that adolescence is definitely survivable—but it's not easy, you remember. So as you're lamenting how difficult it is or is going to be for you as a parent, hopefully you're remembering it's no picnic for your teen, either. When it comes to this phase of life, it's definitely time to cut your kid some slack. We're not talking about giving teens enough rope to hang themselves, but rather easing up a little on the parental end, recognizing how taut teenagers' lives already seem right now because of everything that's going on.

Everything That's Going On

Watching your kid entering into or navigating adolescence can be a real trigger for your own memories, insecurities, angers, and regrets about being a teen yourself. When this happens, your teen's life can become a backdrop upon which you project images from your past onto your child. The problem is, those images belong to you, and only you see them because they aren't really there. If you base how you react upon those self-images, you won't fully know or understand all that's happening with your teen. He may look exactly like you did at that age, but I guarantee you he doesn't feel or experience life exactly like you did. He is unique, and that uniqueness is exactly what's trying to get out during adolescence. If you persist in misinterpreting what you see as merely being a reflection of you, your teen will find himself with no choice but to move further and further from you.

So how do you disengage your own internal feelings and memories of adolescence from what's happening with your teen?

First, you must acknowledge that this process of adolescence is as much a journey of separation for you as it is for your teen. We'll talk about this in greater depth later, but it's important to start thinking about and considering now. As a parent, your identity as a person can become wrapped up in your child. As your child moves through adolescence into adulthood, that identity is going to change because your relationship is going to change. Now is a good time to start looking, really looking, at your teen as more than just an extension or a projection of yourself. This nascent adult is going to be birthed through adolescence with different viewpoints, perspectives, experiences, talents, preferences, goals, and dreams than yours. If you haven't started already learning to accept, acknowledge, and—absolutely wherever possible—approve of whom this unique person is turning into, you're late, but you have some time to catch up.

Second, be prepared for changes. What was true about your child five years ago may not be, and probably is not, true anymore. She may have wanted nothing more than to become a veterinarian at eight, but at thirteen she's determined to be an artist. You were willing to consider taking out a second mortgage for veterinary school back then because at least she'd be a doctor, but now you're not so enthused about her plans of going off to Arizona when she graduates to study art as part of "just living life." Remember, teens are trying on different personas and imagining different futures. This is normal, so throttle back on freaking out just yet.

Third, you need to start really paying attention. About some things, your teen will let you know early and often. About other things, your teen will be much more secretive. It's time for you to take out a rarely used tool in the parental arsenal—subtlety. You will need to become quietly observant. Really listen to what your teen says or doesn't say. Watch the body language; remember, most communication is nonverbal. Again, we'll talk more in depth about this later, but start watching more and lecturing less now.

Bringing It Home

This section requires action. I want you to spend some time thinking about, considering, and observing your teen, especially in regard to the characteristics we've talked about in this chapter. No matter how good you are at observing, whatever you put down is still your interpretation. You need to factor in your own fallibility. As much schooling as I've had in counseling, as much time as I've had in practice, I do not always get things right so I make it a point to remember not to take my word as gospel. Instead, I factor in feedback, self-examination, and reevaluation. I watch and listen and ask questions. I think about my answers and am always a little wary of the assumptions I operate under, especially when dealing with other people. People, especially teenagers, are marvelously complex creatures, but teens are as yet somewhat unformed. They are personalities and people in flux. Your teen is a bit of a moving target so you'll need to stay alert, flexible, and nimble. It's why the old adage says that teens tend to keep you on your toes.

I'd like you to go to a quiet place, away from your teen (depending upon the age, that shouldn't be hard because he or she probably isn't around anyway) and do this next exercise. As easy as it might be to get away from your teen, I'm going to ask you to do something harder; I want you to try to get away from yourself, from that part of you that you tend to project onto your teen. If you're not sure what part that is, hopefully this exercise will also help you begin to see where that might be. You may not have realized it yet, but any book that asks you to look deeply at your teenager must, by default, ask you to look deeply at yourself. The transition from adolescence to adult isn't just for your teenager; it can also be an amazing period of growth and insight for you.

Activity 1: Snapshot

First, I want you to take a deep breath and think about your teen. Okay, capture that image, and hold it in your mind. Got it?

When I asked you to firmly fix your teen in your mind, what image did you go to? What was your teen doing? Was she smiling? Was he angry? How old is your teen in that image? What else do you observe?

Just a word of caution here—you are not allowed to change the image you're holding in your mind based upon the questions I just asked about it. This isn't some sort of parenting test. There is no "right" image of your teen that's supposed to come to mind if you're a "good" parent. The reason this image is important is because the first image you come up with for your teen is probably the strongest one you have right now.

Why is this image the strongest? Is it based on something that happened recently? Is it based upon something you intensely desire or something you deeply fear? Tell yourself why this image is so strong and let it inform you about how you feel about your teen. Why focus so much on you? Because before you can truly see someone else, you need to look first at yourself.

Activity 2: Checklist

The next activity I'd like you to do is to go through teen characteristics as a checklist in relation to your own teen. How do you feel each characteristic relates to your teenager? After you've made your observations, you'll go back and make some notations and differentiations to further clarify what you're dealing with regarding your teen right now. This isn't a timed test so take as much time as you need to think about each characteristic. Allow yourself to acknowledge any anger, frustration, or irritation even thinking about these characteristics produces, but don't allow those emotions to sidetrack you. Stay focused on evaluating your teen.

Some of you will need much more room than is provided here, so feel free to do this on other paper. Some of you are notoriously nonverbal (you know who you are), but at the very least try to write down a word or phrase after each characteristic. I'm not asking you to write a novel, but at least put something meaningful down that you can understand and refer back to. If you need to, go back to the first part of the chapter, where each of these characteristics was outlined, and read them over before you answer for your teen. Again, remember, your teen is unique; some of these may not apply, at least not now.

I would describe my teen as:

O Moody and irritable
O Unpredictable
O Manipulative
O Argumentative
O Withdrawn
O Self-absorbed
O Dramatic
O Dismissive
O Collectively independent
O Anxious
O Powerful
O Exclusively inclusive
O Physically awkward
O Overwhelmed
O Insecure

Now, after each of the characteristics describing your teen, I'd like you to go back and indicate how long you think this behavior or feeling or tendency has been going on. Is it fairly recent? Has it been going on for what seems like forever? Try to quantify a time range for each. Also important is to know whether any of these characteristics is an ongoing trait that is merely exacerbated by adolescence. You may have a fifteen-year-old who has always felt insecure, but it's just gotten worse lately. It's important to know if you're dealing with a phase issue—something that is normal for this age but should level itself out in time—or if there is something more deep seated that will need to be addressed, if it hasn't been already. So go back over each characteristic, and give each one a time range.

Next, I'd like you to go back over the list one more time and write down a single word after each characteristic, describing how you felt as you were writing it down about your teen. If you experienced absolutely no emotional reaction in going over this checklist about your teen, that's a separate issue because most people will have felt some sort of response to thinking about and acknowledging these traits. As I said before, you may have felt angry, frustrated, embarrassed, irritated, put out, exasperated, hurt, empathetic, sympathetic, worried, lonely, disconnected, relieved, appreciative … the list could go on and on.

It's important to know how you react to each of the characteristics that you've identified as describing your teen. You are in a relationship with your teen. How you feel and how you respond matter to and help shape that relationship. Be aware of both as you continue to watch, observe, and become more aware.

Activity 3: Chapter Reflection

This chapter was designed to help you get a better handle on what's happening with your teen. What were the main ideas that really resonated with you reading through this chapter? What caught your eye or captured your attention? They could be insights about your teen or about yourself. What stood out to you? What did you find yourself stopping to read over again? Where in the chapter or in the activities did your mind wander, and where did it go? What did you feel? What did you remember?

Write down three significant insights:

1.

2

3.

It doesn't matter what my intentions are for the above activities and questions; your mind and heart will develop their own insights as you go through them. These insights are so valuable because they will give you important items to focus on and evaluate. Going through this book is work, if you haven't figured that out by now. It is a muscular task that requires effort. I have put what I can into it, but the true benefits to be gained are what you put into it. Treat it lightly, and what you gain will be commensurate. Consider it deeply, and you'll find yourself amazed—not at me but at you and what the work you put into this book can mean for your relationship with your teenager.

3

Emotional Roller Coasters Aren't Very Fun

Veronica scanned the channel listings, automatically rejecting anything that looked like a drama; she had enough of that at home. Sitcoms were out; she simply couldn't stand watching inane banter in a make-believe household. Same with sports; she was trying to get away from conflicts of any kind. Thank heaven for the Discovery Channel and the History Channel; she'd take the burrowing habits of mole crickets or the engineering feats of the Roman Coliseum any day of the week. She wanted escape and nothing remotely related to anything she was going through; although, she had to admit, burrowing had an odd sort of appeal.

She'd just hit her channel of choice when she heard the front door open and then quickly slam. Ahhh, Tyler was home. Let the drama begin. Veronica used to cringe at the thought of teen angst partnered with estrogen and menstruation. But her daughter, Robyn, had nothing on Tyler. Everything was either a crisis or a celebration with him; the roller coaster started when he was thirteen, a little later than with Robyn, but nothing had been smooth since.

When things were good in Tyler's life—completely determined by him as opposed to mundane considerations like outside circumstances—Tyler was on top of the world. He operated at Mach 10, almost airborne. Of course, when he was down, he operated about an inch below the ground, slogging along at a snail's pace, apathetic, dejected, and lethargic. She'd almost gotten used to the weekly swings, but, lately, he'd been careening *back and forth, sometimes multiple times a day. Veronica couldn't keep up; she was so tired of the whole thing, she could feel herself withdrawing from him.*

With a sigh, she realized that just wasn't an option. If he didn't either fly down the stairs on elation's wings or drag himself down within fifteen minutes, she'd go up and try to get a gauge on what was going on now. This was just exhausting. Where was neutral on that kid's controls?

I said before that adolescence is a roller coaster your teen is on, with you along for the ride. Now, don't get me wrong—I like roller coasters. They're an awful lot of fun—if you can really use *awful* and *fun* in the same sentence. The nice thing about amusement-park roller coasters is that you get to choose whether to ride them. They'd have much less appeal if you were forced to ride them even if you didn't feel well or if you were required to keep getting back on as soon as you got off. After a while, the body jerking and the stomach dropping and the head straining would become very old. How do you think your teenager feels about the emotional roller coaster of adolescence? At least you can go read a book or channel surf or take a walk and actually get away for a bit, but teens gripped by adolescence don't always have that option. They are in total reaction mode, and life serves as a huge trigger.

Teenage Children, Not Young Adults

Teenagers are quick to press that they are *young adults* and should be treated as such. That has some validity with older kids, but younger teens are simply not young adults. When you're in the midst of your eighth free-fall plunge in three weeks, this time because he didn't get the part he wanted in the school play or she found out an unflattering picture was posted on someone's Facebook page, I understand the draw, the temptation, for weary parents to want to see the adult light at the end of the teen tunnel prematurely. I understand you can be more than ready for that loopy, impulsive, irresponsible kid to morph into a mature, thoughtful, levelheaded, and, yes, self-reliant adult. *Now,* please.

Not so fast. Teenagers still have a great deal of growing and developing to do. We'll talk about this more a little later on in the book, but, for now, I'd like you to realize that your son or your daughter is not merely a young adult, held back from realizing true adulthood because of a few years of experience or the receipt of a high school diploma. There's more to it than that, as medical research is finding out. If childhood is a time defined by development, then adolescence is still part of childhood because the adolescent brain is in a phase of intense development. A teen brain is not an adult brain.

In the world of research, there is a fascinating technique called *functional magnetic resonance imaging* (fMRI). It's a process that tracks brain activity by monitoring changes in blood flow. The fMRI process shows which different parts of the brain sort of "light up" when activities stimulate use. Through fMRI, you can see how and where the brain is affected by doing all kinds of tasks. With multiple fMRI images, taken from different angles, researchers can actually create a dimensional image of the brain and watch it react and light up. It's really a fascinating science, and it's helped to provide answers to a variety of puzzling questions.

Given the way people have scratched their own heads over the behavior of adolescents, it seems logical that someone, somewhere, would decide to hook up a bunch of teenagers to fMRI and watch what happens. What researchers found was interesting and instructive. I'm not going to get too technical here, but it appears from this study that there is a marked difference between how teenagers and young adults use their brains.[1] When young adults (for this study defined as those between the ages of twenty-three to thirty) and teenagers were asked to perform the same tasks, different parts of the brain were activated. Young adults show changes in the area of their brains used for what are called "executive" functions, like cognitive processing, planning, impulse control, and reasoning. Teenage brains are still developing in that area and tend to make decisions using the part of the brain associated with fear and "gut" reactions. I especially like the final sentence of this article: "While these studies have shown remarkable changes that occur in the brain during the teen years, they also demonstrate what every parent can confirm: the teenage brain is a very complicated and dynamic arena, one that is not easily understood."[2] To which I say, "Amen."

The bottom line, for you as a parent, is to recognize that your teenager is not a young adult but a teenage child, one who is still developing the ability to think and respond rather than simply react. Apparently, researchers could see that around age eleven in girls and around age twelve in boys, mirroring the onset of puberty, preteens' brains got an extra download, if you will, of the type of matter needed to grow and mature in the "executive" functioning part of the brain.[3] However, just because they had the functional capacity to grow in this area, they need the time and experience to learn to use and solidify these new connections. Teens are risky and reactionary, not because they're trying intentionally to push your buttons and make your life miserable, but because those high-reasoning areas of the brain are still developing and will continue to do so into their early twenties.

Researchers at the National Institutes of Mental Health did a study with teenagers and young adults with what they called a "game of chance."[4] Players could choose either a high-risk or a low-risk option. The low-risk option had less reward but greater chance of winning. The high-risk option had greater reward with lower chance of winning. When teens decided which option to choose, they tended to use the reactionary, gut-feeling part of the brain. When young adults decided which option to choose, they tended to use the reasoning area part of the brain. Your teenager may be physically bigger than you, may appear mature, and may feel as ready to be an adult as you are ready to hand over the reins of parenting, but you need to continue being the parent for a few years longer. There's still a lot going on inside, and you've still got an important role to play in protecting and guiding your teenager into adulthood.

Emotionally Afloat

What this means for you as a parent is your teen is being swept along by a sea of physical and hormonal changes, all at a time when he or she is not yet fully anchored in the world of reason, logic, and self-regulation. So be realistic with your expectations. Your teenage daughter may truly have believed that staying out until two in the morning on a school night was the right choice just because her best friend broke up with her boyfriend and absolutely had to talk to her about it right then, and when she says she lost track of the time, she actually did. And when your teenage son comes home with the right-hand fender of your car smashed and an astonished look on his face, he actually might not have anticipated the logical risks inherent in the sport of off-road racing.

There is a sense of invincibility exhibited by teenagers that can drive parents crazy. And what drives parents crazy causes researchers to ponder. The *Journal of the American College of Surgeons* did a study on this very issue.[5] An article on this study concludes the following: "Most teens' attitudes regarding trauma-related injuries, particularly those due to motor vehicle crashes, reflect a sense of invincibility and focus on fate rather than choice."[6] Understanding consequences and outcomes based on personal decisions and choices is a higher-level reasoning function.

Teens often exhibit the classic deer-in-the-headlights look when smacked in the face with things like logic and consequences and outcomes. Forgetting what it was like to be a teenager ourselves, we look at them and wonder, *What were they thinking?!* Seething, we corral them in anger and recite—with clenched teeth and clipped speech—everything they should have factored into their crazy, irrational, even dangerous behavior. Both are, again, classic parental reactions. It's the mother who jerks the child back from stepping off the curb in order to avoid being hit by a passing cyclist. It's the father who rushes in to keep the T-baller from bashing the head of another child who aimlessly wanders into the path of the bat. We know and accept that it's really not fair to expect a five-year-old to have the reasoning power or even observatory skills of an adult. Now, I'm not saying that we ought to treat teenagers like five-year-olds, but I am saying that it's still unfair to apply adult standards of cognizance, reasoning, and maturity to teens, who are simply not there yet. Instead, just as you would for a younger child, consider these teachable moments. It's still your job to stay alert, to guide, and to explain. In this way, you allow your teenager to continue to develop those higher-reasoning functions and mature into his or her young adulthood.

Oh, and it isn't like you can tell them once and have it stick. According to that injury study, even teens who were involved in an all-day risk-prevention program only retained the ability to "identify safer options" for about thirty days. Stronger in their minds was their own set of "evidence": their belief that the design of roads and cars caused crashes; their belief that because of their youth and reflexes they were better able to avoid problems than other drivers; their belief that, because they were young, even if they got in an accident, they'd be able to survive.[7] All of that makes sense to teenagers because their ability to make and retain an adult sense of the way things really work just isn't fully developed yet.

A World of Change

I've spoken before of the black-and-white world of adolescence. Everything is either a triumph or a tragedy. They either love you or hate you. Teenagers are not *nuanced*. They are still learning that the color gray exists in the world. It's why she can come home one day and look at you in horror as you're serving roast beef for dinner because she just watched a video at school about stockyards and slaughterhouses. Yesterday she had two helpings of spaghetti with meatballs, and tonight she's a vegetarian. It's why you get into the same argument with him every weekend about cleaning his room, down to repeating the same lines over and over, as if you're caught in a bizarre temporal loop and you wonder if you're the only one with any sort of memory capacity.

Teens are still in that stage of development where reacting happens more than responding. When you react, it's that same "gut" feeling part of the brain—the world of black or white, of either-or. It's like a switch that's on or off. Your teen is either hot or cold. Sound familiar? It takes all of us awhile to learn how to move past that initial reaction and begin to bring other factors into decisions like experience, consequences, or desired outcomes. It's where something like patience is factored in as an intentional choice instead of a martyred inevitability. Maturity allows elapsed time to become patience instead of merely waiting.

In this black-and-white world of adolescence, where waves of emotion can come crashing down at any time and the anchor of reasoning is not always firmly set, don't be surprised if your teen has trouble navigating the waters. Nowhere is this truer than the realm of relationships. Teens are in the midst of realigning their relationships—their relationship with themselves, their relationship with you as a parent, their relationship with their peers, their relationship with their world, and their relationship with their sexuality. All of that and Algebra 2.

Who Am I?

Before we talk about who teenagers think they are, I'd like you to think about who you are. At what age did you really start to *recognize* yourself? If you could assign yourself a sort of inner age, what would it be? For example, I'm surprised at how many people separate themselves from their outside, older bodies that age, and develop a sense of self disconnected from time. This inner self is often recognized as coalescing into being somewhere in the later teen years. It's when you first came to a significant sense of self. Oh sure, you age, but that inner core—that person you recognize as you—stays somewhat removed from time. People will say things like, "I still feel the same way I did when I was nineteen," or "I still feel like a kid inside." You can look back at this time in your life and recognize how important it was in determining even who you think of yourself as now. This same inner person is forming inside your teenager, and that inner person will solidify and remain long after he or she is past the teens.

We talked earlier about how teenagers, especially younger teens, are trying personas and identities on for size. They are fully engaged in the midst of this same pivotal phase of identifying self, of answering the "Who am I?" question. This is not a question that will be answered fully for many years to come, but the process has begun and continues through adolescence.

In the Bible, Jesus was asked an interesting question by one of the religious leaders of His day. Scripture says this question was asked to "test" Him (Matt. 22:34–35). The question was: "Teacher, which is the greatest commandment in the Law?" (Matt. 22:36). Jesus answered with not one commandment but two, tying them both together. He said, "'Love the Lord your God with all your heart and with all your soul and with all your mind.' This is the first and greatest commandment. And the second is like it: 'Love your neighbor as yourself.' All the Law and the Prophets hang on these two commandments" (Matt. 22:37–40). I have always found it interesting that God ties the command to love other people to our ability, capacity, inclination—whatever you want to call it—to love ourselves. The current phraseology, put in secular terms, is self-esteem.

One of the most important questions that teenagers grapple with during this time of adolescence is, "Who am I?" Then, as they are answering that question, they also have to decide, "Do I love who I am?" Self-esteem during adolescence, as we all know, can take a pretty substantial beating. I believe everyone, whether a teenager or not, really does have a deep need and desire to love who he or she is. Loving who you are is a foundational relationship. It establishes the parameters for so many of the other relationships you have. It absolutely frames this sense of self that is developed through the teenager years.

Loving yourself is not a narcissistic attitude. Loving yourself does not automatically mean loving everything about yourself or loving everything you do. Rather, healthy self-love means accepting and appreciating yourself for who you are. It's what allows you the motivation, the platform, to make difficult changes and to weather seasons of personal growth, realizing who you can become. It can seem that teens are extremely self-centered, which can be interpreted as narcissism. But self-absorption does not equate to self-love in adolescence. Teens are inwardly focused at this time because so much is going on inside them. They, frankly, need to be self-focused; they need to come to grips with these questions and develop healthy answers that will frame their view of themselves into adulthood.

I suppose this question of whether a teenager fundamentally loves himself or herself is not a casual question to me. Sometimes, the answer is life or death, especially in the black-and-white world of teenagers. It's a life-and-death answer for an eighty-three-pound teenage girl trying to find the strength to fight against her anorexia and live. It's the life-and-death answer for a physically abused fourteen-year-old boy trying to put his despair and depression into context and find his way back to joy, without lashing out in any manner of destructive venues. In my practice, I deal with so many of the significant struggles, challenges, and issues people face. The life-and-death aspects to this question of "Do I love who I am?" have immediate consequences for teens.

Other times, the life-and-death aspects to "Do I love who I am?" have longer, lingering consequences. People can live for years with the effects of how they answered this question of "Do I love who I am?" as a teenager. You know this. You know how important this is. A person who as a teenager concludes he or she is not lovable, not worthwhile, has a much harder path to travel as an adult.

Do you remember the visual I gave you earlier about adolescence being like lizards shedding their skin and how uncomfortable that can be? This personal realignment can be the same way—uncomfortable. One minute she likes herself and the next minute she doesn't. One minute he thinks he's a pretty good person and everything's going to be okay, and the next minute he's convinced he's a freak, a social outcast, a lost cause, and all is hopeless. Yin and yang, up and down, climb and plunge with all of the shocks of emotional impact at every twist and turn. Given all of this, there's no way the ride is going to happen without a few bumps along the way.

A couple of final thoughts about this inner "Do I love who I am?" struggle teenagers are in the midst of: This is their struggle. As a parent or outside adult, you can't fight this battle for them. You can support and guide and encourage and persevere, but, ultimately, you cannot answer this question for them. Also, because they are different from you, the way they fight this battle will be different from the way you did. It might be longer or shorter, more visible or more obscure, smoother or bumpier. Their battle isn't necessarily going to look like your battle or their sibling's battle. But all teenagers go through this personal realignment. They need to; it's part of their foundational relationship with themselves, and, frankly, it's one of the most important things they do. So give them space; give them time; give them support.

Struggling teens may need and want to talk to someone besides you, as they work through this question of loving and accepting themselves. They may choose other adults they're familiar with and trust. As long as those adults are truly trustworthy, this is a healthy outreach by your teen and shouldn't be viewed by you as some sort of competition. However, if the adults chosen by your teenager are not trustworthy, you need to intervene. Be prepared to give reasons why you feel the contact is not beneficial, and offer an alternative, including a school or professional counselor.

Who Are You?

As your teenager shifts and realigns how he or she deals with self, this will necessitate a shift in how your teen deals with you. That shift can be seen in the words children use for their parents. Small children start out with terms like *Mommy* and *Daddy* to put a name to who you are to them. At some point, the terms often shift to more "grown-up" terms like a simple *Mom* and *Dad*. Some older children will begin to call parents by their first names or a nickname, which is fine if the nickname is clearly a term of endearment and not used as a derisive substitute.

As the terms and names change, so does the relationship. Teenagers are moving toward a point of independence, as they begin to assume more and more of the responsibility for themselves. As teens are working toward defining who they are for themselves, they are also defining who *you* are for them. Sometimes they get it right, and sometimes they don't.

As people, we live in a world surrounded by our own assumptions. All along, I've cautioned you to be aware of the assumptions you're operating under regarding teenagers—who they are versus who they need to be; where they are versus how far along they should be. You need to realize, also, that teenagers will make assumptions and come to conclusions about you. When they were smaller and less aware, you were just a parental figure. Your identity had a single focus—you were parent as provider. As teenagers mature, they start to notice the world around them and may begin to understand that you are a person in your own right, someone who is a parent, yes, but is also a spouse, a worker, a friend, a volunteer. They begin to ask you about those other aspects of your life and make judgments based upon what they observe, along with what you say.

This can be a difficult transition for parents. Where before you were idolized in some ways, now you are much more critically scrutinized. Teenagers may make value judgments about your choices, your lifestyle, your opinions and ideas. They will often diverge from your pattern of life and thought and explore others. Teenagers are testing; they are probing the boundaries of all of their relationships, including yours.

As they probe, they will question. Often, these questions are not always asked in the atmosphere most conducive for discussion. They can come when tempers are short or patience is frayed. They can come when boundaries are set or weakness is detected. They can come when you're ready and, more often, when you're not.

For teenagers, part of answering that important "Who am I?" question comes from knowing and understanding who *you* are. After all, you have been the most important relationship in their life until recently, when peers climb toward ascendency. You are still extremely important, though they may loathe leaving you with that impression. As they think about who they are and who they want to be, as they try on personas and identities, they naturally look at you and try you on for size. After all, you're the one they've been around the most, seen the most of. In evaluating you, they are going to push against you.

It's sort of like resistance training or isometrics, where you push up against something stable in order to strengthen your own muscles. You're not doing heavy lifting but heavy pushing, using your own weight to increase the load. Teenagers are using you as the stable part to push against. In fact, the only way this strengthening works is for you to remain stable; if you don't, they lose their balance and fall. Getting pushed against all the time isn't really that much fun, but it's easier if you don't take it so personally. When teenagers push against you and decide to go a different way, the message isn't necessarily that you're wrong but that they are being different. They are strengthening their sense of self and their individuality.

Remember, also, that their decision-making processes and capacity to judge whether you are right or wrong are more wrapped up in the reactionary brain than the analytical, reasoning part of the brain. They haven't developed the capacity yet or experienced life enough, in many cases, to see the bigger picture of adulthood. Frankly, after all I've seen over my years in practice, this isn't something I really want kids rushed into. There is something precious and fragile and essential to the innocence of childhood—yes, even the lingering innocence of adolescence. I understand the necessity of grays in the world, but there is something concrete and necessary, at times, in the world of black and white for children.

As your teen pushes against you, he or she is not only strengthening him- or herself, but also getting a better sense of who you are. Teenagers see how you respond; they listen to your answers. Be careful not to interpret your teen's rejection of something you do for a rejection of who you are. Just because he doesn't want to go out for sports like you did or she has no interest in following your career path doesn't mean he or she has rejected you. This can sometimes be the message parents hear, but that isn't what's being said. Just because your teen wants to be different from you doesn't mean he or she wishes you were different. Your teen is saying, *That's fine for you, but I want to live my own life. I know who you are and I love you, but I need to know and be who I am. When I know who I am, I am able to love myself.*

Who Am I with Them?

Paul was determined to stay up, to physically be awake, until Kyle got home. It wasn't easy. He'd stopped paying any real attention to the late-night news show droning in the background about twenty minutes ago. He wasn't as young as he used to be, but when had he gotten so old?

This line of thought wasn't helping, as he waited for Kyle to walk in the door. It just made his irritation grow. It made him mad that he couldn't trust what Kyle was telling him and that he was reduced to this spying behavior. Sure, he could have just stayed awake in his room and listened to what time Kyle got home, but he refused to stay hidden behind his bedroom door as if he was somehow afraid of Kyle. He wasn't afraid of Kyle—he was afraid for Kyle. That was the difference.

It was those kids Kyle had started hanging around with that really had him worried—worried and, frankly, angry. What was he doing hanging around them, anyway? Kyle was going somewhere; half of those kids looked like they wouldn't even graduate from high school. He didn't know most of their names or any of their parents. Where was the respect?

Paul didn't kid himself; it wasn't like when he'd coached the soccer team when Kyle was ten. Then, he'd known all of the kids Kyle hung around with and most of the parents. During middle school, Kyle had changed direction and didn't want to play soccer anymore. To be honest, Paul had been kind of glad, after three straight years of coaching two leagues a year. He was secretly okay with Kyle's decision and hadn't really bugged him about it. Now it kind of bugged Paul. Why had Kyle just suddenly given up something he'd liked so much? Paul hadn't realized how much of their relationship was wrapped around soccer. When that was gone, they'd kind of drifted apart as Kyle got older and Paul had gotten more swamped at work.

Well, it was time to reengage, as far as Paul was concerned. And that reengagement started tonight. He was done just turning off the light, going to bed, and not caring when Kyle came home as long as he was quiet. He didn't like the group of kids Kyle was hanging around with. He didn't like that Kyle wanted to be away from the house more than he wanted to be in it. He didn't like that he and Kyle never seemed to talk anymore. Time was ticking; graduation loomed in a few short years. Paul realized if he was going to make a change, it needed to be now. Paul was sure now was the time to confront Kyle about his friends; he just wasn't sure whom Kyle would choose.

If there is one common thread in adolescence, it's the importance teens place on their relationship with their peers. As they push against you and begin to explore what life looks and feels like on their own, they don't really want to be alone. It is like someone jumping from rock to rock over a treacherous river. There is a perceived danger in being anywhere other than a rock, a place of stability. So teens, at some point, will jump from parents as one rock to other teens as another rock. Other teens, bouncing along that same journey, are often not the most stable of landing places.

Acceptance is a universal need; I've written about it in many of my books, in a variety of different contexts. Acceptance is what teens look for and value in peers—acceptance, which equates to approval and a sense of belonging. They simply do not place the same value in acceptance from parents as they do in acceptance from peers. At least, they don't think they do.

As teens seek to gain independence, they see separation from their parents as a vital component. Even kids who maintain good relationships with their parents will still detach a portion of their lives from their parents. This is the other-life that is generally reserved for their friends and their peers: a peer-life. So teens will naturally develop a home-life, the one they live around their parents, and a peer-life, the one they live around their friends. Being two faced is nothing new to the human condition; you are that way yourself. There is a work-life and a home-life, a professional-you and a private-you. There is the world-face and the church-face. It's what we say over the phone versus what we really comment just after we've hung up. It's the pleasantries we make in public versus the complaints we make in private. We compartmentalize our personalities all the time.

So teens come by this trait naturally. This peer-life is where teens feel free to express themselves in different ways, dress differently, act and speak differently. This peer-life is the experimental-life, the try-it-on-for-size-life. It is where they feel the most provocative, at least in comparison to their child-life. With you, they feel like a child, like the playing field isn't level; with their peers, they feel lateral, running side by side on the same field. This lateral position gives them a greater sense of security to probe, explore, evaluate, and, frankly, make mistakes.

Over and over again, teens will tell me they *absolutely cannot* tell their parents something because they are fearful of their parents' reaction. They will tell their friends, talk about it with their friends, strategize about it with their friends. For something that really scares them or hurts them, they will try to minimize it with their friends and make it go away. Their friends are perceived as safe to tell, while the thought of telling their parents is met with abject terror. Sometimes, this is a reasoned decision, based upon the past behavior of their parents. Mainly, though, this is a gut decision, based on a reaction to fear: fear of exposure, fear of punishment, fear of consequences. Peers are perceived as being accepting of them and their mistakes, while parents are perceived as being judgmental and rejecting.

There is a natural age divide where acceptance comes into play. Teens speak the same language; they understand the same verbiage and slang. They know the same gadgets and apps. They know the same people and are at roughly the same range of development. They are more alike and have more in common with their peers than they perceive they do with you. They have a school-life; you have an adult work-life. You've had mature relationships; they are just starting out. They are young; you are old. They don't want to be lectured to, but that seems to be all you do. They want to be heard but often feel dismissed. You can be tired while they have lots of energy. They are passionate; you can be cynical and disheartened—and disheartening. They want to be told they can have it all; you seem compelled to tell them how hard life really is. They want to live their own life; you seem determined to live their life for them. They want to figure out who they are; you want to tell them who to be. All of this contributes to the acceptance gap between parents and peers, giving peers the decided edge.

Teens are also risk takers. You, as the parent, are the known quantity. They have been around you their whole lives; you are nothing new. Relationship with other kids, however, is exciting and fun. It makes them feel good about themselves to have approval and acceptance from their peers. Oh, you'll do in a catastrophe, like when the timing chain comes off the car and she needs a ride at ten forty-five at night. You'll do when he needs help designing his project and picking up the poster board because the presentation is in two days. You'll do when she's forgotten to turn in her permission slip and it has to be at the school office no later than thirty-five minutes from five minutes ago. You'll do when he's out of money and is absolutely starving. You are necessity; their friends are choice.

This is the point at which parents can be sorely tempted to change who they are in an attempt to relate better to their teens. Feeling their standing slipping vis-à-vis friends, parents can attempt to shift from a parental mode to more of a buddy mode. This is not helpful at all. Do you remember the analogy of resistance training? When you try to shift from parent to buddy, you've removed the stability teens need in order to grow stronger. You are not their buddy; you are their parent. That's a perfectly acceptable identity for you. They will have and go through many buddies and friends during this time; they have only one mother and/or one father. Be patient; you may not know much now, according to your teen, but you will. It's amazing how smart parents get as we get older. I know I've found that to be true in my own life. The older I get, the more my own parents move toward the category of "genius" in so many things. Continue to be the parent, the "genius" you are, and wait patiently for life to reveal that to your teenager.

What in the World Is Going On?

Teens have an uncanny ability to wake up one morning and be intensely interested in things they never knew existed before, let alone cared anything about. This is a natural outgrowth of their ongoing search to the questions in their lives—*"Who am I?" "Do I love who I am?" "Who are you?"* and, *"Who am I to them?"* As their allegiances shift, so do their interests. As they begin to perceive themselves as unique (in other words, separate from you) individuals, the whole world opens up to them. Perversely, one of their first stops along their discovery journey can be one of the many places you've warned them not to go. This searching could—and does—mean all sorts of behaviors, but it also encompasses values, attitudes, and opinions. One sure way for your teen to prove independence is to find a way to push against those things you've expressed value in over the years.

Teens are also adept at sensing and reacting against hypocrisy. Few things are as irritating to them as someone who pontificates publicly about one thing but does the opposite in private. Or people who demand teens follow one set of rules while giving themselves a pass. Teens aren't necessarily thrilled with rules, but they truly dislike double standards. They are reacting against a visceral realization of the vast amount of unfairness in the world; there's so much of it they can do nothing about so they tend to be militant about the stuff they think they can do something about, such as commenting and reacting against your hypocrisy.

When you couple this emergent sense of mission with personal realignment, together with the adolescent desire for peer connection and a systemic rejection of parental status quo, it's not strange that teens would regularly take up the banner of all sorts of causes and groups. Some of these causes can be more benign than others. It's one thing to become part of the group at school collecting blankets and shoes for the homeless; it's another thing to feel a connection to the disaffected within the drug culture. It's one thing to demand equal treatment under school policy for different demographic groups; it's another to join a gang.

Teens have not yet figured out the truth behind the statement "The enemy of my enemy may not be my friend." In a reaction against you or authority or rules or restrictions, teens may align themselves with others who feel the same way, thinking they are like minded. This is one of the most compelling draws of teens who gather together under the banner of drug use. What they fail to realize is that addicts have only one allegiance—and it's to the drugs, not to each other. There are other groups that will take advantage of teens and promise a connection that is surface at best and a lie at worst.

This is why you must remain a steadfast rock for your teenager. You must be and stay the parent. So many other allegiances change and shift, but family remains—once a parent, always a parent. This doesn't mean you'll always have the right to tell your kids what to do; it does mean you'll always have a relationship from which to love your kids. All teens will go off into the big, wide world as they journey to discover who they are. So be aware of where they go and whom they align themselves with. Don't be arbitrary and demanding unnecessarily, out of your own fear. At some point, you want your relationship strong enough that they'll know, no matter where they go, they can always find their way back home.

Who Am I Together?

In this emotional roller coaster of adolescence, each of the previous "who" questions comes with its own particular set of angst, of climbs and falls. Kids who are wondering who they are and whether they like that person can vacillate between delight and despair, based upon a casual comment—positive or negative. Kids can be in constant flux over whether you're their knight in shining armor or their nemesis; whether living with you is paradise or purgatory. Kids who have aligned themselves with an outside group ride the waves of success and failure of that group, either propelling them to elation or plunging them to despair.

If all of these relationship realignments weren't enough to navigate in adolescence, perhaps the most confusing is a teen's relationship with his or her surfacing sexuality. We'll talk more about the physical aspects of this, including sexual activity and teen pregnancy, but handling sexuality alters and affects all of those "who" questions. When teenagers begin to become sexually aware, that awareness can pretty quickly dominate their vision—what they see, how they see, what they think about, what their priorities are. Because of the intensity of sexual connection, these relationships have the potential to send teens on their wildest rides ever, with you right along with them, both of you hanging on to sanity for dear life.

Andrea was trying to be patient. After all, it was Jessica's first time being "dumped," and Andrea knew all too well what that felt like. In fact, it was hard not to drag her memories into the whole situation. Part of her wanted to call over to Matt's house and give him what for. But that wouldn't be helpful. Matt wasn't obligated to continue dating Jessica; they were just kids. But the pain Jessica was feeling—the pain Andrea was feeling for her—felt more like adult pain than kid pain.

Why did it have to be so hard? Should she have put her foot down and kept Jessica from dating until she was a little older? Would that have made it better? Of course, if kids wanted to go out together, they could. They had all that time at school, and Andrea didn't GPS her daughter's cell phone to make sure she was exactly where she was supposed to be all the time. She didn't creep her or her friends on Facebook; she refused to sink to that level of intrusion into Jessica's life. So even if she'd said "no dating" for another year, she couldn't be sure this wouldn't have happened anyway.

How long was too long? How much crying was normal? Jessica had been a zombie for over a week. At first, she said she'd had the flu and couldn't go to school. When the crying was too loud to hide, she'd finally admitted she was sick because Matt had broken up with her. That was the first time in a long time Jessica had allowed Andrea to just sit and hold her. She'd had one brief moment of needing her momma before adolescence reasserted itself and she'd pushed her away again.

At least Jessica wasn't still crying all the time, at least not that Andrea knew. Now, she just spent hours on the phone with her friends, gaining comfort there instead. Every time Andrea tried to broach the subject to see if she wanted to talk, Jessica made it abundantly clear the situation was off-limits. Jack, plainly, was keeping out of it, delegating this sort of issue to her as the resident female. So she waited and she worried, and she remembered too clearly what it felt like to have your heart ripped out through your throat. She'd survived; Jessica would too. Knowing that made it only a little easier.

We'll spend chapter 5 going over the physical/hormonal aspects of adolescence, but I mention it here because romantic relationships are tailor made for the all-or-nothing, black-and-white world of adolescence. The emotional impacts of other relationships can seem like the kiddie loop-de-loop at the neighborhood carnival; these relationships have the capacity to send your teen careening down an emotional track akin to the tallest, steepest ride at Six Flags Magic Mountain (it's called *Goliath* for obvious reasons, and it's a huge, steel monster).

This kind of sexually focused roller coaster isn't merely for those who are in a romantic teen relationship; those who want to be in such a relationship are also caught up. The thrill of hope and the plummet of disappointment can send your teen on this wild ride. Sometimes the most painful experiences are felt by those who never are asked out on a date, who won't be going to the prom, who desperately want to be noticed and appreciated by someone romantically but never are, or, worse, are only noticed as a source of derision and ridicule. This intensive emotional and physical imperative unrealized during adolescence leaves its own kind of scarring. It can complicate a teenager finding healthy answers to all those "who" questions.

In short, your teenager is going to be an emotional being for the next several years. Wishing otherwise is fantasy. If it's not over his relationship with himself, it will be over her relationship with you. If it's not about his relationship with his peers, it will be over how she fits in with the world at large. If it's not about her dating, it will be about him wanting to date.

So be prepared to ride it out. Be prepared to be patient. Later on, we'll go through a whole chapter on that sort of parental preparation, but for now, just recognize this as the new reality for your life. Wishing your teen were something other than who he or she is isn't going to help. Wishing your teen would be more like you or his sister or her cousin isn't going to help. You need to acknowledge and accept your teen for who he or she is right now. Your focus needs to be laser sharp because, as the parent, you have an invaluable role to play. You cannot answer your teen's "who" questions, but you can provide as stable and as loving a platform possible as your teen seeks the answers to those questions for himself or herself.

Oh, and one more thing—the ride will end. By the grace of God, your teen will at some point move from adolescence to young adulthood. There is something exhilarating after getting off a really scary ride, like the Goliath roller coaster. It's definitely not for the faint of heart, and there's a kind of implied courage given to all who ride it. Just watch them at the exit gate the next time you go to the fair or an amusement park. Rides are just rides, but the analogy, I think, still holds. Valuable things, though difficult, are worth doing well. My prayer is that both you and your teen will have the same sense of shared experience, smiling together with satisfaction and accomplishment at the end of this ride, even if your hair is a mess, your glasses are askew, and you don't feel like eating lunch anytime soon.

Bringing It Home

Are you a Merry-Go-Round person or a Roller-Coaster person? That's an important question to ask yourself as you evaluate this chapter. Merry-Go-Round people like solid, steady consistency in life. They aren't really much for change and certainly not for rapid change. They like slow, steady, and predictable. Roller-Coaster people find slow and steady dull and boring. They like the white-knuckle thrills of the spontaneous, of the unknown. It's exciting and energizing.

I'd like you to determine—overall—what kind of person you are: Merry-Go-Round or Roller Coaster. This has implications for how you approach life during this turbulent teenage time and how you parent. There are advantages and disadvantages to both, in a general sense.

Merry-Go-Round parents will be the most disturbed emotionally by the topsy-turvy ride of their teenagers. They will experience the most discomfort and may experience resentment over the chaos their orderly lives have been thrown into. That's the disadvantage. The advantage of being this type of parent is the steadiness and stability they can provide in a time of crisis. Calm and determined, even plodding, they are able to see, often, what needs to be done and can plot a path to get there. They are the organizers, the planners, the plodders. Because they are firmly grounded, they can provide an anchor point.

Roller-Coaster parents can thrive during the ups and downs of adolescence because this is a normal state of being. It can be an advantage because they have an innate understanding of how teenagers think and feel. They don't get as queasy about the ups and downs of adolescence as the Merry-Go-Round parents. This is the advantage. The disadvantage in being this type of parent is the combination of the volatility between parent and teen. Emotionally demonstrative and thrill-loving—even thrill-seeking—parents don't always provide the best input, guidance, and grounding that an impulsive teenager needs. If the parent isn't really thrilled with being and acting like the parent, this disconnect can create a void when a teenager really needs a parent.

If you are a Merry-Go-Round person, how does this affect your parenting, both positively and negatively?

If you are a Roller-Coaster person, how does this affect your parenting, both positively and negatively?

Understanding that teenagers really need balance during this time in their lives, what is one way you could ease up a bit on either the Merry-Go-Round or the Roller Coaster in your own life?

4

Shaky Connections

Angela could feel the stress building and her anger rising exponentially. Not again! Why did Valerie always seem to put her in this position? She had enough crises in her own life; she didn't need more of Valerie's drama too. Angela could feel herself shutting out Valerie's frantic explanation of why she hadn't gotten the project done earlier and why she had to have Angela's help right now.

The worst part, Angela knew, was that she had no real choice. It was about school, and Valerie knew how important that was to her. So she'd just have to forget whatever else she'd planned for the next two days because Valerie's crisis was sweeping everything else off the table.

With a clipped tone and barely contained fury, Angela went into "fix it" mode. Seeing the switch, Valerie adjusted too, going from why she needed her help to what needed to be done. She immediately became cooperative and compliant, relieved to find out what sort of rabbit Angela was going to help her pull out of her school-project hat.

They went round and round over three different possible solutions, evaluating each, considering what they needed and the amount of time left. Decision made and list in hand, they headed out the door to pick up supplies. Relief made Valerie almost giddy, and she chatted excitedly in the car on the way.

As Valerie talked, Angela realized anger wasn't the only thing she was feeling. It was anger and frustration and resentment, but there was also a strange sort of satisfaction, too. Valerie needed her again, like when

she was little. It had been a while since Angela had been able to have
that Mom feeling—needed, relied upon, and, honestly, wanted. For the
brief time of this crisis, Angela wasn't being pushed away by Valerie; she
was being embraced, in a frantic, stressed-out, desperate sort of way. So
while Angela hated it, she realized she kind of liked it too. It was a weird
time of life.

It is, indeed, a weird time of life, always changing and more than
a bit unsettling—shaky, even. Get a group of parents of teenagers
or preteens in a room, and one of the common themes that will
come up is this yin-and-yang, hot-and-cold, on-or-off switching that
teens do when it comes to how they relate to you as a parent. If
everything's going fine, you're extraneous. If things are going badly,
you're somehow partially responsible. If things are going really
badly, you're supposed to swoop in and fix it. That's not really a
comfortable position to be in.

If you were dealing with another adult, you might be tempted to
blurt out that old adage about how it's up to the person who jumped
into the water to sink or swim. But this isn't an adult; it's your child.
A teenager, yes, but still your child, and the last thing you want is
for him or her to go under. You're still responsible, at least legally, for
several more years. You're also still absolutely affected as a parent by
that child, no matter how many years go by. Your children's crises, by
extension, will be your crises; there's no getting around it.

You and your teen are connected through relationship, a relationship that keeps shifting on what seems like a daily basis. As a
parent, this time of life can make you feel relationally motion sick.
Even though your connection with your teen is twisting and turning

so much you'd really like to get off the ride for a while, you've got to hang on. Just because it's shifting and changing doesn't mean you can't provide some stability on your end. You've got to; you're the adult.

Because you're the adult, we're going to start by focusing on you, the connection point you are in the relationship with your teenager. In order for a good connection to be established, both points of that connection need to be working. Your car battery may have plenty of juice, but if your cables or posts are compromised, your car isn't going to fire well or sometimes even start. In your relationship with your teen, you need to know if there's been some corrosion on your end, interrupting a good, solid connection.

I think one of the hardest things about this time of life is that we parents live within an illusion of control. We like to think we've got a handle on our lives, our jobs, our kids. We like to think we have a handle on those things that are the most important to us, those things that, really, have the capacity to cause us the most pain. For us parents, our children are at the top of the list of those things that can cause us pain. So control is very important. The teenage years take that illusion of control and attempt to throw it right out the window. It's why parents of teenagers have so many sleepless nights and unsettled days from a who-are-you-now, what-are-you-going-to-do-next, what-am-I-going-to-need-to-do-in-response parental anxiety. Teenagers are an unpredictable component in a controlled adult world. You think you know them, but do you? You think you've got a handle on what they might do or need or say, but do you?

Which brings me to something that is used often by recovering addicts, who need to learn to adapt to a changing environment. (And if parents of teens need to do anything, it's to learn to adapt to this changing teen environment.) It's called the Serenity Prayer. Probably the most commonly known version is this: *God, grant me the serenity to accept the things I cannot change; courage to change the things I can; and wisdom to know the difference.*[1]

Interestingly enough, there are different expanded versions. One I really liked says, *God, grant us the serenity to accept the things we cannot change, courage to change the things we can, and the wisdom to know the difference* (so far, so good)*; patience for the things that take time, appreciation for all that we have, and tolerance for those with different struggles; freedom to live beyond the limitations of our past ways, the ability to feel Your love for us and our love for each other, and the strength to get up and try again even when we feel it is hopeless.*

I was stuck with how appropriate this expanded version was for parents of teens. Each phrase just spoke to me.

Patience for the things that take time. Like waiting for thirteen-year-olds to turn into twenty-five-year-olds. Like awaiting the restoration of some semblance of sanity in your home. Maturity is as elegant and captivating as any butterfly emerging from its cocoon during chrysalis. It can be hard to compare the stately and colorful beauty of a monarch butterfly to your gangly, pimply teenager, but, I contend, the metaphor remains valid. Instead of comparing your teen to the butterfly, go back a few steps and remember your adolescent is more like the pupa—the wormy, sometimes slimy, often weirdly and disturbingly colored pupa. You won't get to the beautiful butterfly part until a few years down the road, so don't rush the analogy. You both will get there—it's just going to take a little more time.

Appreciation for all that we have. Can teens be irritating and time consuming and frustrating? Yes. But I know of families that lost children before they reached this disturbing age, and I will tell you they would give just about anything in this world or the next to be able to complain along with the rest of the parents of teens. Your teenager is a gift to be grateful for.

Tolerance for those with different struggles. As we've talked about before, you will share many of the same struggles with your teen, but some of the struggles will be different because every person is different. Difference requires understanding and tolerance.

Freedom to live beyond the limitations of our past ways. We're going to park on this one in just a bit, but I want you to start to consider what sort of limitations on your relationship with your teen may exist because of your past ways.

The ability to feel Your love for us and our love for each other. One of the things parents and teens both express doubt about during the teen years can be the love they have for each other. Parents feel marginalized, excluded, discarded, and unloved by ungrateful teens. Teens feel pressured, judged, separated, and unloved by frustrated parents. The capacity for misunderstandings and harmful words is rife during this time. It's why parents truly need the ability, through it all, to remember and feel the love they have for their teenagers.

The strength to get up and try again even when we feel it is hopeless. With the drama and struggle and stress of raising teenagers, sometimes it can seem hopeless. You're sure that kid is never going to graduate or change or learn or just plain mature or get a job or have a clean room. You're worried you're going to be stuck with that slimy, spiny pupa and despair of ever seeing even a hint of the butterfly.

Nothing you say or do seems to have any effect (except to make you both madder), and you feel like you're butting your head against the brick wall called Adolescence. That's when you need the strength to get up and try again even when you feel it is hopeless.

Past Limitations .

Carl wanted answers. But he didn't want them here. Not in front of all these people and certainly not now. He wanted answers, but, more, he wanted out. He'd never been in this part of a police station before, and it didn't help that it wasn't about him. It was just plain stupid behavior! Now he'd have to spring for an attorney and get this cleared up. The school was involved; great—was there anyone in the neighborhood who wouldn't know about it? Hardly. It was probably being tweeted up and down the block already. His kid, involved in this—Carl shook his head in utter disgust.

They brought Austin out, his face expressionless, just doing what he was told. Carl couldn't tell if he was overwhelmed or shut down or both. Again, it wasn't the time to figure it out—just get out and figure it out later.

As unpleasant as this was, Carl knew it was only the beginning. He wanted answers, but he didn't really want all the answers. Answers to why Austin hadn't confided in him earlier, let him know the trouble he was in. Answers to why Austin would do this in the first place. Carl had a feeling there was more to this story than he wanted to hear and more than enough blame to go around.

Part of this version of the Serenity Prayer asked for the *freedom to live beyond the limitations of our past ways.* I mentioned I wanted to expand this thought, and I do so with a warning: This section is not going to be easy. It's really easy to identify all the crazy stuff your teenager does that drives you nuts and irritates you and causes definite strain in your relationship. It's less easy to identify how you complicate and bruise and cause tension in that same relationship. It's easier to see that sort of thing in others than it is to see in yourself. It's the plank versus speck in the eye talked about in Scripture. Jesus explains it this way in Luke 6:41–42: "Why do you look at the speck of sawdust in your brother's eye and pay no attention to the plank in your own eye? How can you say to your brother, 'Brother, let me take the speck out of your eye,' when you yourself fail to see the plank in your own eye? You hypocrite, first take the plank out of your eye, and then you will see clearly to remove the speck from your brother's eye." Now, read the passage again, and this time, substitute the name of your teenager for "your brother."

I'd like you to consider whether limitations of your past ways may have formed a plank in your eye, as you look at and relate to your teen. The connection with your teen through these years can be shaky enough, but some of the anger and sense of being overwhelmed you feel may come, not because of your teen, but from you. So before you can clearly see your relationship with your teenager or what needs to be done for or by your teenager, you may need to engage in a little plank removal.

I don't think there's much I do as a father that's harder to admit than when I've hurt one of my kids because of my own past limitations, faults, failures, or sins. As much as I wish I could say I don't do this, I do. I hate it, but hating it doesn't prevent me from hurting my kids because, like the apostle Paul, when it comes to my kids, I sometimes do the very thing I do not want to do (Rom. 7:15). Yes, it's hard to admit, but because we're talking about teens and how frustrating a relationship with them can be sometimes, I thought it only fair to factor in what you and I do to damage an already fragile teen relationship.

The first thing you need to do is recognize that a shaky relationship with your teen is not always about your child. Sometimes, it's about you. As parents, each of us has a past. That past includes all the mistakes we have made up to this point in our lives, including those we've made as parents. Who you are as a parent didn't spring forth anew as your child entered adolescence. It might have changed at that point, but there was already a baseline relationship that had been established during all those years of parenting that child. It's difficult enough to weather the ups and downs of your child's adolescence when you have a pretty good relationship before puberty starts. What do you do when the struggles of adolescence highlight preexisting relationship difficulties between you and your teen? How do you try to batten down the hatches of a troubled relationship while you're in the midst of an adolescent gale?

Some of the challenges you have with your teenager now may stem from baggage you've been carrying around from your past—past hurts, past relationship failures, past personal challenges that predate your teen but over the years have come to adversely affect your relationship. These challenges may have always been a part of that relationship; it's just that your mouthy, independent, belligerent, no-holds-barred teen has simply reached a point of adolescent frankness and decided to call you on them. As I said before, teens detest hypocrisy and double standards and may finally have reached a point in their lives where they're willing to call you on the personal shortcomings and limitations you bring to the table as a parent. They are, after all, prone to impulsive, ill-thought-out actions. So the very thing you hope they never do—speak a terrible truth about you—may be the one thing they decide to do out of their own anger, frustration, and pain.

Are you ready for that as a parent? Are you ready to take a look—from your teen's point of view—at your own limitations and what those have meant to your ability to parent? One of parents' terrors is having their teenagers' behaviors call attention to their own inadequacy as parents and, perhaps even more so, as people. It is as if your teenager has the capacity to undress you in public, to expose you as a parent and as a person. They can, and occasionally they will. Over the years, I've seen some parents react well to this exposure and others react poorly. These reactions have huge ramifications in the lives of teenagers and in their subsequent relationships.

Reacting Poorly

We live in an "I'm fine" world. No one expects everything or everyone to be perfect, but I believe there's a reason why "fine" is a universal response to the question of how you're doing. Fine isn't saying you're great or you're perfect (because that would be boastful and bragging and would draw attention to yourself)—but you're fine. It's a way to answer the question while forestalling any deeper probe. It's a way of answering the door and shutting it again, all in the same word. Parents who live in an "I'm fine" world generally act poorly when private things are exposed by their teenager's behaviors.

Teens can be notorious for revealing family secrets, especially the personal secrets some parents so desperately want to stay hidden.

They do this in a couple of different ways. They can do it by their words, by talking about what is wrong with their lives, including their family-life and their life with their parents. They can also do it by their actions. A troubled teenager, acting out away from the privacy of home and the control of parents, clearly demonstrates that everything is not fine with the family and, by extension, the parents. Parents who react poorly to this exposure tend to place total blame on the teenager, refusing to admit any responsibility in the troubled relationship and resulting behavior of their teenager.

As an aside, notice I said responsibility and not blame. I'm not really focused on fixing blame; I would rather determine responsibility. To me, blame is something bestowed upon you by other people; responsibility is something you take upon yourself. When you take something upon yourself, I believe you have a better chance of finding a way to improve, to mature, and to do better. Blame, to me, is a dead end, while responsibility has embedded in it a pathway to improvement.

Again, parents who react poorly choose to make their teenager solely responsible for the difficulties he or she is experiencing, from trouble communicating, to anger outbursts, to academic difficulties, to other issues like stealing or sexual promiscuity or substance abuse. These parents are resistant to family counseling, to seeing or understanding what role their own attitudes, behaviors, or parenting may have played in the situation. In a desire to deflect blame, they reject any responsibility and end up leaving their teenager adrift.

Every parent, myself included, no matter how diligent or well meaning, no matter how learned or educated, is not going to be perfect. We're going to mess up as parents, unintentionally and even intentionally, because we're not perfect. And when we do, our kids get hurt. Hurt teenagers do stupid things out of anger, fear, and frustration. They can choose outrageous and dangerous ways to demonstrate their pain.

There is another way parents react poorly when their teenagers act out. Instead of rejecting any responsibility, some parents take on all of the responsibility, thus removing it from their teenager. Again, if there is one thing teenagers need to know and understand, it is that actions have consequences. Teens do not have this intuitively or cognitively nailed down yet and won't for several years so they need concrete reminders.

So you have a sort of Goldilocks situation—accepting none of the responsibility for your teen's challenging behaviors can be like the porridge too cold. Accepting all of the responsibility for your teen's challenging behaviors can be like the porridge too hot. To react well, you need to find someplace in the middle, where the truth lies.

Reacting Well

Parents who react well accept their own responsibility in their teenager's challenges, difficulties, and failures. They don't try to minimize their teen's part in the behavior, either. They are able to find a path through to the reality of things. Teens need to have that path demonstrated over and over again. They need to understand and have a healthy respect for the truth, even when it is uncomfortable. As a parent, you model that by respecting the truth about yourself and your parenting, by accepting that your teen will bear the consequences of your weakness as a parent. This means, of course, that you don't get to choose your weakness. You must accept the areas of personal weakness that are revealed through the life and challenges of your teenager, not only the weaknesses you feel comfortable admitting.

Expect to be surprised. We cover over and rationalize our weaknesses, especially those that carry the most fear and shame. Our camouflage is pretty good at obscuring the truth when we look at ourselves in the mirror, but it doesn't usually extend to our kids. They see and react to the weaknesses we pretend don't exist. It is why mothers who have debilitating weight and body issues they've been covering over and rationalizing for years find their own daughters caught in the throes of an eating disorder. It is why fathers who, out of a fear of failure and inadequacy, have traded in family and relationship for professional success find their own sons discounting and discarding their lives through substance abuse. It's why parents who have consistently put off spending time and making their own children a priority in their lives find those teenagers are only too happy to cut them out of their lives and growing independence. Your teen has lived with you a long time and has seen the things you don't show to others. This is the fundamental reason why to be a parent is to risk exposure as a person. As I said before, teenagers have a way of exposing family secrets. When that happens as a parent, joining your teenager in the truth has to be more important than the personal pain and embarrassment of exposure.

Creating Stability

Some of you may wonder why this particular chapter on connection, on relationships, has turned into such a focus on you as the parent. That is because in relationships, the only person you really have control over is you. To paraphrase Scripture: If it is possible, as far as it depends on you, live at peace with your teenager (Rom. 12:18). You establish the peace, and you do that through stabilizing the relationship from your end regardless of what your teen does. You must become the port in the storm for this sometimes turbulent relationship. You take charge over yourself first by understanding and accepting the ways you've contributed to any difficulty in your relationship. You take charge by apologizing and making an honest effort to do better. You model by removing your own plank first and then bringing up specks. Teens don't expect you to be perfect, but they'd appreciate a little honesty, especially where your faults are concerned.

Of course, sometimes your teenager is just going to baffle you with his or her leave-me-alone, I-need-you-now adult-child switching behavior. You'd like to just throw up your hands in frustration and ask plainly, *What do you want from me today?* Instead of disparaging your teen's shaky connection with you, seek to cement that connection, no matter in what form it appears. And be patient. Be flexible. Your teenager will reveal how she is feeling about herself and how he views himself through interaction with you. The important part isn't whether he or she connects with you as a grown-up kid or an underage adult; it's whether he or she continues to connect with you in the first place.

The firm foundation your teenager needs is you as a parent to be clear about who you are and what your role as a parent is, even when that role is confusing and frustrating. There is a real danger here, if parents decide to abdicate their role as parents during the adolescent years for something else that feels more comfortable. Many of these situations, taken to extreme, are outlined in my book *Healing the Scars of Emotional Abuse.* Teenagers who are cheated out of that childhood role and thrust into another by a parent suffer a form of abuse.

The parent-child relationship can become warped during adolescence, essentially creating a role reversal where the parent begins to look to and expect the teenager to fill the parent's needs. It is not healthy for you to begin to look to your growing teenager as someone to fill your adult needs. These can be adult needs for companionship or camaraderie, even advice and protection. Adolescence is meant to be a process for teenagers to grow and mature into their own person, filling their own needs, not yours.

I have seen mothers, afraid of their own aging, begin to morph into older, distorted images of their teenage daughters, even wearing similar clothes and adopting similar hairstyles.

I have seen fathers, fearful of their own aging, treat their sons as peers and demand their sons reciprocate, requiring time and attention to the detriment of same-age friends.

I have seen mothers, fearful of the coming empty nest, bind their teenagers to them through increasing demands and intentional displays of incapacity.

I have seen fathers, troubled and discontent with their own lives, transfer that negativity onto their teenagers, dragging them down just at the point of launch in order to experience companionship in failure.

I have seen parents burden their teenagers with the weight of their own fading dreams of accomplishment.

Granted, these examples are extreme and produce an unhealthy attachment and enmeshment, a sort of relational strangulation.

However, I say this as a reminder to all parents. Adolescence is a time of discovery and possibility for teenagers. It can also come at a time of disappointment and a sense of loss for parents, because of the juxtaposition of age. Aging parents can become fearful of advancing time and look to their teenagers to help slow the march. Solitary parents can become fearful of being left alone and look to their teenagers to fill the gap. Angry, embittered parents can look to teenagers as an outlet for venting and release. Maybe these examples aren't you, but please be aware and willing to look inside yourself to see if any of them claim even the smallest place in your heart.

Teens are growing into their potential at a time many adults may feel their own potential waning. This can cause jealousy and envy and contribute to the tension and friction between teens and parents. These sorts of issues have the capacity to damage and sever your connection with your teenager, without you even really understanding why. As you enter into this pivotal time of transition, I encourage you to make sure you hang onto your identity as a parent so you allow your teenager to retain his or her identity as child for a few more years.

Establishing Connection

This chapter has mentioned different ways your teen can relate to you—either as a standoffish, I-don't-need-you, underage adult or as a clingy, help-me-now, grown-up kid. There is actually another way your teen can relate to you, and that is not at all. Teenagers have the ability and the option to disconnect from their parents entirely. They may not do it physically for a few more years, but they can certainly do it emotionally and relationally right now.

If your relationship is too troubled, too complicated, too stressful or painful, your teen may decide to stoically ride it out, knowing that time is on his side and that he'll eventually be out on his own and gone. If your relationship is too smothering, too judgmental, too negative or controlling, your teen may decide to reciprocate in anger, allowing herself to feed off it until she finds someplace else to live and someone else to love.

If your teenager cannot connect with you on a relationship level or if that relationship is too stressful, painful, or difficult, there are plenty of other places your teen can connect. Even if your relationship is merely strained and not broken altogether, your teen has plenty of options for connection, validation, acceptance, and support apart from you.

You are in a competition for your teenager's connection. You are competing with peers and with technology because many of those other options for connection are only a cell phone or keypad away. It used to be that you punished a child by sending her to her room. Now, that may not bother him at all because it just means he can communicate all he wants with whomever he wants, without your knowledge or interference. Just because your teenager is in your house, in his room, doesn't mean he's alone.

Most teenagers have cell phones. A current study by the Pew Research Center says that 72 percent of them do.[2] Of those kids who have one, 88 percent of them use it to text.[3] Texting, not email, has become teens' preferred means of communication.[4] This means that cell phone you provided as a way to keep track of your teenager or for your teen to have in an emergency is also one of your biggest competitors for the affection of and connection to your kid. If teenagers don't feel they can connect with their parents, they'll link up over the cell phone with someone else.

I think most parents would be surprised by how much connecting their kids are doing over those cell phones. Here are a couple of the summary points from that Pew study, which I encourage you to read:

- Teens are more apt to text their friends than call them up and talk to them.
- Of the vast majority of teens who text, over half of them send fifty or more messages per day. One-third send more than one hundred messages per day, and 15 percent send more than two hundred messages per day.
- There is a difference between girls and boys when it comes to texting. Girls send and receive an average of eighty messages per day, while for boys it's an average of thirty messages per day.
- Teens do more with their phones than just text or talk. They also take pictures (83 percent) and share those pictures (64 percent), play music on their phones (60 percent), and play games (46 percent). They go online (27 percent) and access social networks (23 percent).[5]

Teens say they like texting because it's easier and more convenient than talking. In other words, they are in charge of if they text, what they text, and when they text. Interestingly, teens say they will avoid answering their cell phones in order to train people to text them instead of call them. This has forced parents to take up texting, even when they don't really like it, because it's the only way to get their teens to answer them back. It also means that if a teen has a cell phone, he or she has access to other people, to other connections. Fifteen percent of teens say they've gotten a text message with a sexually suggestive, nude, or nearly nude picture of someone they know. *Of someone they know.* This isn't surfing general porn; this is intentional, directed sexual pictures of someone they know sent to them. In a room of a hundred kids, that's fifteen of them with those kinds of pictures on their phone. How many kids are in your teenager's class at school? Do the math.

All of this is happening on a device so small they can carry it in their pockets, a device with the ability to be set on silent so you never know it's ringing, a device supplied by parents whose primary reason for getting it is safety. Welcome to our brave new world.

This is just one recent reason to add to the age-old mix of reasons why it is so important you maintain a connection to your teenager. You are going to have to be like a tenacious rodeo rider. To me, navigating this time of transition is like being on the back of a bucking bronco. You're going to do a lot of shifting and moving in order to stay ahead of the twists and turns of your teenager. There are times you're probably going to feel like losing your lunch, but you've got to hang on. You've got to be the parent and stay the parent. You've got to keep the lines of communication open and available.

Be aware of how you're reacting to your teenager and why, including reasons that have nothing to do with your teen and everything to do with you. Avoid the tendency to blame, and look

for ways to understand what and who are responsible for difficulties in the relationship. Come clean about your own past mistakes
and shortcomings and work toward forgiveness. I'm not talking yet
about forgiving your teenager; I'm talking about you. Seek to forgive
yourself, accept responsibility, and take positive steps to change and
improve. It is an amazing phenomenon that once you are able to
forgive yourself, it is easier to forgive others. Remember, you are still
your teenagers' role model in what it means to be an adult. They may
outwardly dismiss you, but you've been center stage in their lives
since they were born. You may have been knocked down a notch
by their friends, but you're still vitally important. You're still the one
they're going to come running to when they realize they've messed
up and have only two days left to finish that project at school. When
they're in trouble and need help, you want to be the one they connect
with, no matter the personal cost.

Bringing It Home

I'd like you to create your own personal Serenity Prayer. Either type
out or write down thoughts about or create an art piece around
the expanded Serenity Prayer from this chapter (be as creative as
you want!). At the least, type the expanded Serenity Prayer out on
a piece of paper, and keep it where you can see it. If you want to
dig a little deeper, use it as part of your artistic expression. Here is
my own rendition, in an "I" format:

God, grant me the serenity to accept the things I cannot change, courage to change the things I can, and the wisdom to know the difference. Give me patience for the things that take time, appreciation for all that I have, and tolerance for those with different struggles. Give me freedom to live beyond the limitations of my past ways, the ability to feel love—my own, Yours, and others'—and the strength to get up and try again when I feel it is hopeless.

Next, I'd like you to separate out each line of that prayer and write down or think about what it means to you personally, in regard to the connection you have or would like to have with your teenager. This is something you can incorporate into your copy of the prayer or just something you can have as a reminder of what each line means to you.

5

This Is Your Body on Adolescence

Over twenty years ago, there was an amazingly effective public service announcement by a group called Partnership for a Drug-Free America. It was effective—not so much because it caused a dramatic decrease in the use of drugs, but because this one short ad seared itself into the collective cultural consciousness. I remember the ad vividly. There was a man in a kitchen. He held up an egg and said, "This is your brain." He picked up a pan and said, "This is drugs," and put the pan on the stove. Cracking open the egg, he dropped it in the pan while saying, "This is your brain on drugs," as the egg fried and bubbled. He looked at the camera and said, "Any questions?" Fade to black.

It was a graphic representation of a complex and difficult reality—the effect of drug use on the health of your brain. Up to that point, I'm not sure people had given much thought, as a whole, to what drugs actually did to a person's brain. Sure, they could see the physical effects on a person's body, on their demeanor and behavior, but the brain was sort of a mysterious, shrouded object that most people didn't truly understand unless they were in a medical or research profession. That ad brought into focus drugs and what their use was doing to the brains of thousands of people. And the message was simple—drugs fry your brain. Easy to grasp. Easy to remember.

Fast-forward to today. You, as a parent, can see the physical effects of adolescence on your teen. You observe their demeanor and behaviors; you remember your own. But puberty and adolescence have been sort of mysterious, shrouded by a process you don't truly understand unless you're in a medical or research profession. Frankly, it's a process many of us tried very hard to just survive as teens and then to hunker down and survive when it's our kid's turn.

But reverting to this hunker-down-and-just-survive-it mode for adolescence is a cheat. Surviving isn't really experiencing life to the fullest, and there are parts of this time of life you'll want to fully experience. Remember—the slimy pupa morphs into a beautiful butterfly in time. You wouldn't want to be hunkered down so much you miss it.

Do you remember the discussion in chapter 3 about the research breakthroughs regarding imaging of the brain? And about how different adolescent brains are from even young adult brains? There is so much going on in the brain of your teenager. There is so much going on in the body of your teen directly connected to that brain. While you may become focused on the physical changes you can see and experience every day, don't forget there's a lot going on "upstairs" as well.

Health Class 101

The name of this brain-body connection is puberty, and the key is hormones, the seeming lifeblood of every teen. Now, I don't want to return us all to the thrilling days of yesteryear when we sat mortified in health class, wishing we could somehow fade into invisibility, but it's impossible to understand teens without talking about sex and its unique hormonal stew. Your teen, during adolescence and through the process of puberty, is becoming a sexual being. This is a game changer—your child is becoming a sexual adult and realizing the potential inherent in gender.

In Genesis 1, the Bible says, "So God created man in his own image, in the image of God he created him; male and female he created them" (v. 27). I like that verse because it combines both the concept of singularity (mankind) with the concept of duality (male and female). Aren't people just people? Yes, we are all part of mankind. However, we are different; we are male and female.

I remember growing up in a weird time when the differences between male and female were intentionally downplayed as a way to achieve gender equality. People were to be considered androgynous in everything except physical body parts. Any substantive differences between the sexes were viewed as environmental and cultural, not genetic or inherent. It was a sort of one-sided version of the "people are people" mentality, with everyone supposed to think, act, and learn the same. Gender differences were muted, and any mention of them hushed and frowned upon, as if you'd belched during a funeral.

Thankfully, that phase of "there are no real differences between girls and boys" didn't last long, as cultural concepts go—certainly not more than a couple of decades. Now that it is permissible (at least in many circles) to openly discuss the differences between girls and boys again, there is a tremendous amount of research going on—research that clearly demonstrates that, yes, there are significant differences between boys and girls. These differences are not only in how their bodies mature but also in how their brains develop. (If you really enjoy research articles, you could browse through "Sexual Dimorphism of Brain Development Trajectories during Childhood and Adolescence,"[1] or "Sex-Related Developmental

Differences in the Lateralized Activation of the Prefrontal Cortex
and Amygdala during Perception of Facial Affect."[2]) There is just
a wealth of research out there, all providing quantifiable data to
what parents have known pretty much all along—girls and boys
are different.

This Is Girls on Adolescence

*After being on his feet for the last three hours, all Gordon wanted to
do was find a nice, quiet bench and sit down. Of course, that wasn't
an option. Under other circumstances, this simple request would seem
logical, but they were on vacation, and Peggy had made it abundantly
clear they were going to take full advantage of every second. But it was
the Smithsonian, for heaven's sake! You could literally walk around for
days and not see all of it. That hadn't deterred Peggy in the least, nor
did it appear to deter Rachel, who was going strong, practically jumping up and down with excitement, chatting nonstop with her mother.
They were supercharged after three hours; it was Gordon who lagged.*

*Watching the two of them, walking and talking without a break,
Gordon felt more than a little left behind. In some ways, he mused, they
were like joined twins, Peggy and Rachel, joined in their femaleness.
Taking a closer look, he could even see the physical similarities in their
figures. Rachel was wearing a blue T-shirt, one that actually showed
her shape, instead of the baggy hand-me-downs she generally favored.
Startled, Gordon realized he could see a definable waist and hips.* Wait
a minute, *he thought to himself.* When did that happen? How old was
she? *All of a sudden his fatigue was overcome by something akin to panic.
With a start, he realized he was watching two females walking ahead of
him—one a woman and one about to be.*

Girls hit puberty about two years, on average, before boys. We're all pretty familiar with the physical changes happening to girls during this time so I won't rehash those. If you're the parent of a teenage girl, you're already fully aware of how and how fast she's changing physically. You wish she'd slow down because you're not sure she's ready for it, and you're absolutely sure you're not. But if you thought the only things you needed to factor into your daughter's adolescence were finding the right bra or figuring out what kind of feminine hygiene product to buy, you're going to need to expand your horizons. There's a lot more going on inside even than there is on the outside.

Girls are able to connect to their emotions more quickly than boys. In fact, they often can discuss *how* they are feeling *while* they are feeling it. In adolescence, this allows girls to be fully present in the moment, but they can also get caught up in that moment. This is real-time emotional impact without the benefit of hindsight, which sets the stage for the sort of all-or-nothing drama so indicative of a teenage girl. It's a crisis because it feels, right now, like a crisis, and she's overwhelmed by the power of that right-now emotional force. It's why she can go from the delight of having you come at the end of school to pick her up to the disaster of having that hot guy from English actually see her getting into a car with a *parental unit* all within a matter of seconds, before you've even gotten the transmission out of park.

As a parent, you need to keep a calm head and refuse to respond emotionally in kind. This isn't a personal repudiation of you as a parent; it's a normal reaction to being embarrassed because her carefully crafted persona of adulthood and independence has been shot down by the harsh reminder that she doesn't have her driver's license yet, let alone a car, and your presence is proof she's not really as grown up as she'd like to appear. Allow the crisis to pass without reacting to it and stoking the fires. After all, it's not really about you.

Emotional Expression

Girls are more verbal. So if she's in the midst of an emotional crisis—or it really feels like it—you're probably going to hear about it. Girls are able to remember details and put emotionally connected elements into their speech. This means you'll know exactly what she's thinking and why, if she chooses to talk to you. She may keep up a private, running conversation-argument-debate-harangue in her mind and choose not to share it with you, at least out loud. She may choose to express herself through writing down her thoughts instead of verbalizing them or verbalizing them to peers instead of to you. Just because she isn't saying anything doesn't mean she isn't thinking anything.

However, if your teenage daughter is in the midst of an emotional episode and she does choose to express herself to you, she may say things that are pretty raw—things she hasn't really taken time to consider because she's actually processing them as she's speaking. You're not going to get the edited, for-parental-consumption version, in other words. So instead of hearing in a measured, calm tone how disappointed she is that you've failed to fully evaluate the logic behind her request to spend the night at Sara's, you'll simply hear her scream that she hates you at the top of her lungs.

Upon reflection, she will admit that, no, she doesn't actually hate you but that she hates the way it feels when she isn't able to do something she really, really wants. And she hates not understanding why you can't see something she sees so clearly. And she hates being left out. And she hates having to tell Sara that her parents wouldn't let her because, again, it reminds everybody of the fact that she is not the detached, independent person she so desperately tries to present but is, in fact, still a kid. And she hates being seen as a kid when what she really wants is to be seen as an adult. So she doesn't really hate you; it just comes out that way.

Emotional Memory

Girls have emotional memory; in other words, girls can not only remember an event, but they remember how they felt during the event. The power and impact of an event are sheathed in her memory within its emotional context. A teenage girl becomes a historian, remembering events, situations, and circumstances, especially when there is pain or hurt involved. This emotional coloring can actually distort the reality of a situation, turning perception into truth. So yes, she will remember the conversation you had three weeks ago about her taking the car to the away football game. However, she may remember it quite differently because you said no instead of yes.

It's not going to work to try to talk her out of how she feels. She feels what she feels. Instead, your only option is to allow her the time to remember the details of the event, gently worked away from the emotions. This isn't invalidating her emotions; instead, it's framing the event in a different context—in your context—and allowing her to experience the event afresh, without her emotional layering. This is really a high-level reasoning skill, the kind adults need and use all the time. She's not yet ready to be a pro at this kind of reasoning, but it's very good practice for her to start considering other points of view besides her own when thinking about events and context. This is important adult practice, but don't expect her to master this skill overnight. Give her space to learn, which means you may simply have to agree to disagree without resolution for a while. Be patient.

Emotional Connection

Girls are able to connect with the emotions of others. Teenage girls are attuned to what other people are thinking and feeling—so attuned that other, lesser details may be overlooked or forgotten. It's why she can spend an hour on the phone going over a friend's breakup in minute detail but appear put out and rushed when you want to go over the chore list for Saturday.

She may not show it, but she's also able to connect with how you're feeling. If anything, she will be especially attuned to the adults in her life who hold the power of things like permission to go to the mall on Saturdays or having a friend stay over. Of course, she may only use this remarkable gift of emotional clairvoyance to figure out the right time to approach you for ten dollars or a new pair of shoes.

Recognize that she's probably going to be awash with emotions—either her own or others'. All of these emotions can constitute an overwhelming flood, and she may occasionally find herself gasping for air. This may make it difficult for her to concentrate on daily things like chores and homework or even saying "good morning" and "good night."

As much as she may fight against it, doing mundane, ordinary things is probably very good for her. Loading the dishwasher or walking the dog is hardly exciting—and that's the point. It allows her to reestablish her rhythm and process things on a subconscious level, apart from any additional emotional context. So don't be upset if she doesn't do them exactly like you want. And don't let her off the hook for her chores, thinking she's not up to them. She is; she needs something to do while she sorts through this wash of emotions. She may not be doing it the way you want, but she's actually engaged in something more important than folding the kitchen towels.

Juggling

Girls are good at multitasking. In adolescence, this can go into overdrive. She'll have so much going on at one time, it stresses you out even to be around her. She'll be talking on the phone, scribbling in her notebook, glancing at her laptop, all while listening to indiscernible music. Your concept of calm, of peace and quiet, is foreign to her. It is why, yes, she'll go to the movies with you, but she'll text right up to the reminder not to do so before the movie and as soon as it's done, without considering you might possibly find this behavior dismissive and rude. In her mind, she can do two, three, even four things at once and, frankly, would rather—because she can—and it's fun—and what's the problem?

Yes, she's good at multitasking, at juggling a variety of activities and thoughts, but even the best juggler drops balls if they're too big or too many. Watch how many she's juggling and how big—not so you can rush in and take over but so you'll be available when the balls inevitably come crashing down. She needs to learn balance and how much she can handle; she can't do that if you're always moving her aside and trying to take over. In order to learn how it works best for her to succeed, she's got to learn how to handle it when she fails.

Primary Relationships

For girls, relationships are everything. The good news is she will factor in her relationship with you and with other adults, like peers' parents and teachers. However, as we talked about before, for adolescent girls peer relationships are primary. This means if she has two hours in which to be with friends or get that world-history project done, it's going to be a real toss-up, depending upon what's happening with her friends. The obvious to you will not be the obvious to her because of this peer priority. If you point out that the world-history project should take precedence over spending time with her friends, she may accuse you of marginalizing how important her friends are to her and won't recognize the logic behind completing her schoolwork.

For a teenage girl, relationships are everything, but romantic relationships are air and breath and life. The physical changes hardwired into her anatomy are designed to produce sexual feelings and desires. She wants to be with boys. She wants to be important to boys, to be noticed by them. She wants to be considered physically attractive to boys.

Most teenage girls want to be in a relationship with a teenage boy. Whether she is or not is determined by a variety of factors, some in and some out of her control, but the desire to be in a relationship is fairly universal and compelling. If she is not in such a relationship, she will spend time attempting to be in one or thinking about it. How she relates to and is seen by boys at this stage of life is crucial to how she will feel about herself as an adult woman. It is at this stage that so much can go right for her, and so much can go wrong.

The frustrating part for you as a parent is she may not tell you how she is feeling as her sexuality emerges or what is happening relationally with the males in her life. If she has a boyfriend for any length of time, you'll probably meet him, but you will not be privy to everything that happens within that relationship. She will keep a good deal of it private and share it only with her peers, if at all. While she may make sure you know exactly how she feels about her third-period English teacher or your no-friends-over-on-Sunday rule, she may be uncharacteristically mute on her emerging sexuality.

The obvious danger of all this privacy and secrecy, of course, is that an adolescent girl may not be emotionally or intellectually or relationally ready, but she is physically ready to go from girl to mother. So even if she does not tell you how she's feeling, you have got to make it very clear how you're feeling. You need to explain how you feel about teen sexual activity and why. She needs reasons, not just rules.

There's so much more to this than just sitting down with her and having The Sex Talk. By the time she's thirteen, it's a little late to go into the differences in plumbing. What she needs to hear is your validation of her as a sexual person. She needs to hear you have confidence in her ability to control her own behavior and to make good choices. She also needs to hear what you consider good choices to be.

Even though teens have access to an overwhelming amount of information about sexual activity, remember they may not yet have developed the cognitive ability to wade through all that information and make the best choices. They are still governed by impulsivity and peer pressure. They are also exposed to rumors and falsehoods about sex and about how to prevent pregnancy. Your teen needs to hear the truth from you. Make sure, however, before you discuss sexual issues with your teenager that you've done your homework.

Find sources you trust and become familiar with sexual issues, terms, behaviors, and consequences. Teens will ask others about what you've said, whether they ascribe the information to you or not. They need to know that you're speaking the truth and that you're speaking your mind and your values. Above all, you need to communicate your love and acceptance of your teen. Too many teens turn to sex as a substitute for those two key ingredients in their lives.

A word to fathers: Your daughter entering puberty is not the time for you to decide to turn over parenting to her mother because her emerging sexuality makes you uncomfortable. This is the time she needs you more than ever. Believe me when I say she can tell if you're uncomfortable and may interpret that as a rejection of her emerging sexuality. She may believe you think there's something wrong with her. Her relationship with you is the primary male-female relationship she has had up to this point. It needs to form a strong foundation for the male-female relationships she's going to form in the future. We'll talk about this more in a later chapter, but please be aware that your reactions matter to her more than you could possibly imagine. I know because I spend a lot of time with women, adolescent and adult, who mourn this loss of relationship with their fathers, even years and decades after the fact.

This Is Boys on Adolescence

Once I saw a great illustration of the difference between men and women. It was grossly simplistic, of course, but like all great illustrations, it captured the core of so many things in a single image. Actually, there were two images. The first image was of a rectangular box. It was completely covered in dials, knobs, levers, and latches. The heading on the image was "Woman." The second image was of the same rectangular box—but with only a single on/off switch in the middle. The heading on this image was "Man." I remember laughing out loud when I saw it because, on so many levels, I found it to be true. It encapsulated a fundamental difference between girls and boys:

- Teenage girls want to know *why*. They are emotional, verbal, multitasking, abstract thinkers. The "why" of things is often complex, detailed, and circuitous—well suited to a female brain with the number and speed of its neural connections.
- Teenage boys want to know *how*. They are concrete, compartmentalized, reactive, and in-the-moment thinkers. The "how" of things is often physical, kinetic, and spatial—well suited to a male brain with its ability to focus and capacity for risk.

You will remember that I talked about that strange time in my youth when the culture promoted the concept that there were, basically, no differences between male and female, outside of the plumbing. Again, thankfully, that didn't last long, but it was replaced by an equally pernicious and destructive concept—that there were, indeed, differences between boys and girls … and girls were better. It's not my goal here to reargue this concept or go into all of the cultural reasons why it became prevalent. Instead, I mention it because it continues to echo in the cultural consciousness.

Are there differences between girls and boys? Yes. Is one superior to the other? No. Difference does not equate to hierarchy. Frankly, all of this current brain imaging research not only fascinates me but also vindicates what I've experienced over my career as a therapist. Men and women are different: They see things from different angles; their reactions and responses to the same things are sometimes radically different; and each one is empowered and enhanced by understanding and appreciating the point of view of the other.

If you have both a teenage boy and a teenage girl, don't expect them to act identically. And even when they act the same, don't expect their motivations or impulses or reasons behind those identical actions to be the same. Your teenage boy is different from your teenage girl. He is going to act, react, think, and feel differently. And that's perfectly normal. Teenage girls grow up to be women; teenage boys grow up to be men. Different—so why shouldn't the process by which they get there be different?

Response Time

Going back to our on/off box analogy, the differences between boys and girls come down to two main areas: Boys tend to cognitively respond more slowly but physically respond more quickly. What this means is girls may be the first ones to raise their hands in a class but boys may be the first ones to raise their fists in a fight. Looking at the first, boys take more time to process and respond to information. In a girls-are-better worldview, this makes boys appear slow and somewhat dim witted. But speed of decision does not necessarily equate to value of decision.

I remember counseling a woman who was experiencing marital difficulties after about ten years of marriage. She loved her husband but found, increasingly, that she had little patience for what she perceived to be his entrenched flaws. One of the things she was most irritated with was his tendency to "ignore" her. She considered this an invalidation of her feelings and opinions. I asked her to give me an example, and she mentioned how he appeared to be resistant to answering her when she asked him a question, even a simple question. It got so bad, she said, she started counting the seconds in her head it took him to respond. If he didn't respond within a few seconds, she assumed he was ignoring her or had "tuned" her out. So she'd ask again. Each subsequent request carried greater emotional weight. She felt ignored; he felt verbally attacked. These exchanges were becoming a significant source of conflict between them.

I suggested to her that perhaps he wasn't ignoring her; I said maybe he just needed more time to consider what it was she'd said and come up with an answer. I also suggested that if she asked him a question when he was in the midst of doing or thinking about something else it might take him a little bit longer to detach from that in order to consider what it is she'd said or asked. He wasn't intentionally trying to ignore her; he simply needed more *time* to answer. I asked her if she was willing to exercise a little patience and wait for him to respond with his timing instead of demanding he conform to hers.

The results of her patience were immediate. She came back a week later and reported she'd been amazed. At first, she admitted she fought with the same feelings of invalidation and rejection when he didn't respond as quickly as she thought acceptable, but she began to see those feelings as coming from her and not him. Over the next several months, by giving him the time he needed and removing the pressure to come up with an immediate response, the air of conflict receded. A simple question went back to being a simple question. A conversation went back to a congenial give-and-take.

Boys simply need more time to cognitively process information, especially verbal information. What this means for you as a parent is that your teenage boy can become overwhelmed by an oral onslaught. About thirty seconds into your five-minute verbal download on your frustrations over his lack of care and concern over his physical space (i.e., his room), he is probably going to assume that deer-in-the-headlights look. While you pontificate over every example of disarray, ticking each one off with meticulous logic and articulation, he will probably remain speechless, affecting a "What are you talking about?" incredulity. You've probably already figured out that this approach just doesn't work well.

Physicality

Boys are more physical than girls. They move more; they need to move more. Physical movement helps them order their world, including their emotional world. They are also spatial thinkers; they are more aware of themselves in physical space. They can extrapolate spatially and envision the manipulation of objects in physical space. This allows boys to recognize and identify patterns. They are sensory, visual, and tactile. They learn better by doing than by hearing.

Boys tend to react physically to how they're feeling emotionally. If they're confused or frustrated, they're going to fidget. If they're excited, they're going to gesture. If they're angry, they're going to pound or kick or punch. If they're wound up for any reason, including positive ones, they're going to physically move. Because they can become so physically charged, it can take them longer to "wind down."

Boys tend to take longer to move mentally from task to task. Girls tend to be jugglers—keeping multiple balls in the air all at the same time and moving from ball to ball much more quickly. Boys are ball gazers; they have the ability to fixate on a single ball and maintain that sense of focus. They are able to appreciate how it looks from all sides and how that ball affects their world. If they're concentrating on that one ball, other balls in the air around them are apt to get dropped.

Boys are competitive. This competition is all-encompassing and can include a variety of venues, from winning the game on Friday night to taking the girl out on Saturday. It can be as important as winning a regional academic competition to as trivial as who gets to the locker first. Boys will also compete against themselves, often using unrealistic standards to evaluate their own performance.

Boys are risk takers. They are possibility thinkers. They have fewer reasons not to do something and a greater belief in their own abilities to succeed, especially in physical arenas. They can be impulsive and optimistic. They are less apt to ask *why* and more apt to conclude *why not*.

Concrete Recall

Boys are concrete recallers. Girls tend to attach much more emotional and sensory detail to their memories, thus making the feelings associated with those memories come alive. Boys remember what happened but are not as tied to how they felt when it happened. This doesn't mean boys don't have feelings when things happen—just that their memories are not as connected to those feelings. Boys may not *feel* the same way about an event as a girl does or may have a harder time recognizing a connection between a current feeling and a past event.

So let's go back to the teenage boy with the not-just-messy room but the whirlwind-of-destruction room. A five-minute verbal tirade on the fact that it's messy generally won't produce the kind of results you want, especially if it's launched right after he's come home from soccer practice and all he can really think about is what's available to eat. He's been out running for an hour and a half and now he's home and that room is just perfect, as far as he's concerned, as long as he can bring a glass of milk and a bag of chips in there with him until dinner is ready. For the past hour and a half you've been fuming about the wretched condition of this pigsty of a room and all you can think about is he's finally home and it's about time he took responsibility for its unacceptable condition, especially when you just talked to him about it three days ago and it's no better and probably worse. He thinks it's perfect; you think it's a disaster. You want to discuss it with him, but, with boys, remember *timing* and *presentation*:

- Wait until after he's at least had something to eat. If the world hasn't ended in the past ninety minutes, since you looked in there and decided you'd had enough of his slovenly ways, it's probably not going to, so you've got a little time.
- Then, after dinner and before he starts into whatever else he's got to do, let him know you want to talk to him about his room. Give him advance

warning about the timing and the topic so you're both on the same page before you begin. You're telling him he needs to pick up the ball that is his room and think about that.

- Next, ditch the lecture. Condense your comments to a few concrete statements, and allow him to respond to those. This way, the lecture becomes what you really need it to be—a discussion. You want him to understand your position and accept your point of view. He doesn't equate the condition of his room with your level of frustration and condemnation. Keep it concrete; the focus should be on a mutually agreed upon room condition, ideally, or at the very least what your definition is, as the parent.

- Control your emotions. Yes, you may be completely put out, frustrated, and angry, but yelling, screaming, and verbal put-downs are not going to produce the results you want. These may be interpreted as an attack, to which he may respond in anger and physically. This is just his room; it doesn't need to provoke a "fight or flight" response, but it can, especially with a volatile teenage boy.

- Move around in the physical space. Don't just talk about the fact that he never puts his clothes in the hamper; walk around the room and use physical examples. Have him pick up items strewn around and determine if they are clean or dirty. Reiterate the concrete rule: Clean clothes are put away properly; dirty clothes go into the hamper. Yes/no—on/off.

- Let him know you're on his side, that you trust him to be able to understand and accomplish these few simple goals. You do not want this to become some sort of heated competition between you, because he'll be more than happy to tell you to "bring it on." You don't need a teen who is revved up over dirty socks. However, he does have a competitive side, and he may respond to the challenge you've presented.

- Keep it short. One or two examples will do. This isn't quantum physics. Get him physically moving and then give him his space. You've set the standard; now give him time to accomplish the task.

- If you're still emotionally stressed and have a need to vent, go take a walk or engage in some other rote activity. Give him his space and time to respond.

- Show appreciation. Just because he doesn't transmit his need for your approval and acceptance doesn't mean it isn't there. It doesn't have to be much, but it does need to be expressed.

- Keep him accountable. Consequences can still be a foreign concept to him, one that needs to be fortified. Cleaning his room and keeping it clean are a simple way to reinforce the truth that *actions have consequences*. If his actions don't produce the consequences you've outlined, how is he to learn this vital lesson?

Sexual Charge

As much as it would be a relief to just have to deal with teenage boys and their messy rooms, there's so much more for you to navigate as a parent. Boys may mature later than girls, but the differences don't end there. Teenage girls are focused on the emotional/sexual charge they get from a relationship; teenage boys are focused on the sexual/physical charge they get from that same relationship. It is impossible to understand teenagers, boys included, without coming to grips with this sexual component. It is not necessary for boys to be in a relationship to experience that sexual/physical charge from girls. They just need to be around them.

As a parent, you need to be alert to this need because it can lead teenage boys into areas they should not be going, including pornography. With the power of visual stimulation, pornography is a huge issue for boys and, frankly, adult men. It is powerful, addictive, and destructive. It is anonymous and immediate. Online, it's amazingly accessible. On their phones, it's amazingly personal and provocative. As the parent of a teenage boy, you need to be aware of the draw sexual visual images have. It may not be a discussion you feel all that comfortable engaging in, but it is one you need to have. Again, you need to make your own feelings, opinions, and, yes, rules very clear regarding having and viewing pornography, whether print or digital.

Your teenage son is becoming, just like your teenage daughter, a sexual being. Ready or not, some will take their sexuality to its physical conclusion. The government's Centers for Disease Control (CDC) tracks a vast amount of data on behaviors and conditions, including teen sexual activity. In a recent report, "Teenagers in the United States: Sexual Activity, Contraception Use, and Childbearing, National Survey of Family Growth 2006–2008," the CDC research showed 42 percent of teenage girls and 43 percent of teenage boys experienced at least one incident of sexual intercourse.[3] It is a sobering publication that I encourage all parents to be aware of.

Teenage girls can become mothers and teenage boys can become fathers, both long before they're ready. A teenage boy may not carry a child physically, but he will carry that child emotionally for the rest of his life. He needs to know, just as much as your teenage girl, what you think and why. How you feel about his messy room is an important discussion to have, but it pales in comparison to this one. Make very sure you have both.

Physical Support

Whether you have a teenage girl or a teenage boy, there's a lot going on physically in that body and brain. As a parent, you can create some simple physical conditions to help support your teen's maturation process. These are commonsense items you already know about but may not have made a decision to implement for your teenager (or yourself, for that matter). In some ways, I feel like a broken record (for those of you who remember what a record is), but I've been stressing them for people I've worked with and in my books for decades. They're not complicated, but they aren't necessarily easy, either:

- Eat healthy.
- Get plenty of exercise.
- Take nutritional supplements.
- Drink lots of water.
- Get plenty of rest.

I can anticipate your reaction where your teenager is concerned:

- Eat healthy—*Are you nuts? I don't know what he's eating most of the time. I never see it. If I offered to pack him a lunch to take to school, he'd accuse me of treating him like a child. The only thing he seems enthusiastic about is pizza; I swear he could eat that every day and be happy.*
- Get plenty of exercise—*The only exercise she gets is walking up and down the stairs to her room. She says she hates to sweat and refuses every offer to go for a walk or to do anything physical, like mowing the lawn. When she takes the dog out, it's only because she's crazy about him, but, even then, they're back before ten minutes is up, and she complains about him pulling her the whole time.*
- Take nutritional supplements—*Yeah, right. He can't even remember to bring his homework to school half the time. There's no way I want to become the*

Pill Police, trying to stuff supplements down his throat like some current version of cod-liver oil.

- Drink lots of water—*Oh, she gets plenty of water, all right; it's just in diet soda. Water is her beverage of last resort. Water is something you take a shower in, according to her, not something you drink.*
- Get plenty of rest—*He's too busy to sleep. According to him, sleep isn't something you get every night; it's something you catch up on during weekends. Bedtime is a sort of activity purgatory, a forced exercise in sensory deprivation. It's a state of nonbeing that needs to be kept at bay for as long as possible and eased into with music playing, at the very least.*

I do understand what you're going through, and I appreciate the challenges involved here, but I still want you to work to make headway in each of these areas anyway. Your teenager needs to develop these healthy habits not only to get him or her through adolescence but also to have these habits firmly established for adulthood. Youth, after all, doesn't last forever. The body may be forgiving at fifteen; it is less so at fifty.

You have more influence than you know, and now is the time to use it, especially while your teen is still living under your roof. Each of these areas doesn't need to turn into a battle royal; you just need to set your course and stick with it.

Eat healthy. While most teens eat at least one meal away from the house, they are probably getting the majority of their food at home, at least several days a week. This is where you can start. Make sure there are healthy alternatives available for them. What you have in the fridge and the cabinet is what they have available. Teens are notoriously convenience driven.

Make your selections palatable. There is a greater variety than ever before of healthy and good-tasting food. There's nothing wrong with a light cheese sauce on broccoli or ranch dressing with carrot sticks or peanut butter with apple slices. Put some thought into your selections; if you won't eat them, neither will your kids.

Start whittling away at the junk. There's nothing wrong with a package of cookies in your cabinet, but if all you've got in there is four different kinds of cookies, three packages of chips, two types of crackers, along with premade frosting and prepackaged cake mixes, there's an issue. The cabinet should not be the first place your kid goes for food; ideally it should be the refrigerator, where fresh fruits and vegetables are kept. I understand it's a process, so why not start by removing a nutritionally unnecessary item and replacing it with a healthy one?

Be proactive about aiding your teen's choices. He may not want you to pack his lunch, but she may appreciate that there's a bag of carrots cleaned and ready to go in the fridge. She may still hunt out the cookies when she gets home from school, but they could be your homemade whole-wheat raisin cookies instead of a package of chocolate marshmallow wafers. Convenience is important to a busy, distracted teen, but convenience doesn't need to mean prepackaged.

Realistically, the two meals of the day you're going to have the bigger influence over are breakfast and dinner. For breakfast, look for something healthy, and make sure you've always got it around. Breakfast is not so much a meal as it is a ritual; people tend to eat the same thing for breakfast and tolerate uniformity at this meal more than at any other. Help your teen establish a healthy pattern, and sheer routine will do the rest.

As much as possible, for as many days during the week as you can manage it, have a sit-down healthy dinner with your teen. Can it be pizza occasionally? Sure. However, your general meal should include lots of vegetables, fruit, whole grains, and lean protein. Dinnertime shouldn't be a culinary creation chock full of fat, salt, and calories, meant as a reward for surviving the day. It's your dinner table; use it well.

Get plenty of exercise. For parents of younger teens, this is easier because physical education is still part of most middle school curricula. In high school, however, it can become more complicated with elective choices like bowling. The type of exercise your teenager needs is cardiovascular and, ideally, should be vigorous enough to produce a sweat. Some high schools allow kids to waive out of PE in order to take other electives or needed requirements. If this is what your teen is experiencing, exercise is going to have to come through a different venue. It might need to be an after-school sport. It could also be your teen getting out and moving on his or her own, via bicycling, walking, or running. It could also be indoor, virtual exercising on a game system, a stationary bike, or an exercise or dance DVD. Also, don't be deceived that a thin teen is a physically fit teen; the two can be very different things. Appropriate exercise is beneficial for everyone, not just for those who are overweight.

You're going to have to get creative for those kids who are not already involved in sports. And even if your teen is involved in some sort of organized sport, there's nothing wrong with establishing a

habit of exercise, just for its own sake, not associated with any organized team. Otherwise, once the season is over or the team is history,
the exercise it provided may be equally left in the dust. Daily exercise
is a valuable habit that is easier to begin and establish as a teenager
than it is as a much-older adult.

Take nutritional supplements. We're not talking here about a
dietary cornucopia of horse pills. Instead, just help your teen start
the habit of taking a good multimineral, multivitamin each day. Talk
to your teen about the best time and place to take it, so it will be
remembered. Teens have access to so much nutritional information,
more and more of which is coming to them during school. You may
be pleasantly surprised at how easy it is to get your teen to agree.
After all, in the vast array of things you require them to do, this really
isn't such a big deal, especially if you're taking one yourself.

Drink lots of water. Okay, you're not with your teen all day
so this one is going to be difficult. My suggestion is to get one
of those water purifier jugs to keep in your refrigerator. No one
likes to drink lukewarm, foul-tasting water. We are blessed in the
Pacific Northwest to have some of the most satisfying, good-tasting
water I've ever had. It comes out of the tap refreshing and cold. You
may not be so fortunate so you'll need to simulate those conditions
artificially. Make the water easy to get and the other stuff harder
to find. Buy your teen his or her own water bottle to carry around.
Go to the trendiest teen store you can find, and ask the teenage
clerk for suggestions. If you can't pick out the right shirt, you're not
going to come close to the right water bottle. Ask for help because
you want them to actually use it, not throw it under the backseat
or at the bottom of their backpack.

Get plenty of rest. You cannot stand over your teen and monitor sleep. That's just not realistic—but you can create an atmosphere at night in your home that invites relaxation and calm, especially as the evening fades into night. This means it's a good idea to ask at 6:30 p.m. if homework is done instead of 8:30 p.m. This means turning off lights and turning down electronic devices instead of having an artificial noon in every room with music, television, game stations, computers blaring at full blast. Also, when teens are recharging, so should cell phones.

Teens need a lot of sleep because of the complex physical changes their bodies are undergoing. This is at direct odds with the teen lifestyle that seems determined to emulate adult late nights, while still maintaining a 7:15 a.m. school schedule. Your teenager may be functioning on six hours of sleep during the week and then staying in bed until early afternoon on weekends, but this is not physically beneficial. Our bodies work best within a wake-sleep routine, one that doesn't vary too much. Too little sleep places stress on the body and on its major systems. A fatigued, grumpy adolescent is not a happy camper—he's not able to function at his best and feels terrible. Do your whole family a favor and make the evening in your household a time of transition toward relaxation and sleep. There is growing evidence that teens physically function better getting up later and staying up later, but until school and work schedules shift to accommodate, you and your teen will have to do the adjusting.

Earlier we talked about higher-reasoning brain functioning. If there was ever a way for you to practice these skills with your teen, it's over these five simple guidelines. Each one of them requires you to see beyond the instant gratification of unhealthy choices and grasp the concept of future benefit. Each of them requires perseverance and dedication to implement. Again, these don't need to turn into self-righteous lectures or the latest "get healthy" fad. Rather, if you believe and implement each of these in your own life, you'll have a firm position upon which to make your case for family-wide implementation. As we noted before, teens are notoriously suspicious of do-as-I-say-not-as-I-do. You're not going to get away with carrots and apples slices for your teen while you're eating doughnuts and cookies.

Give your teen some credit and start a dialogue. Be honest and open about the changes you want to make and why. Admit your own struggles, when appropriate, but don't burden your teen if you have considerable food/weight baggage. Your teen shouldn't be made into your diet companion or your food police or your weight counselor. That's what people like me are for. Believe me, the last thing you want to do is transfer any or all of that baggage over to your kids.

Realistic Expectations

Whether your teen is a girl or a boy, adulthood is not going to spring into being in them overnight. It is going to be a years-long process. Your patience will be needed and tested. Your teen's patience will be needed and developed. It's a process you must go through together but also separately. Don't bring unrealistic expectations into this volatile time. Accept that your teenage boy is going to maneuver through this process on a different path than your teenage girl will. Avoid the tendency to compare, contrast, and make value judgments on the differences. Learn to celebrate the differences and appreciate them for the diversity they contribute to the human condition. We don't all have to be the same. We are allowed to be different, and that difference enhances us—it doesn't diminish one over the other.

Live and model this in your own life and attitude. Do your part for your teenager. Be there. Be calm. Be patient. Be accepting and open. Be loving and forgiving. The butterfly part is coming. You want your relationship with your teenager to survive intact so you can see that butterfly part and appreciate it together.

Bringing It Home

Growing up, what were three things you remember being taught about the differences between males and females?

1.
2.
3.

For each one you listed, try to remember who taught you that or where you learned it. Did you ever have any reason to question this male-female lesson as you got older? What about now—do you still think that way?

Reading over this chapter, what do you think about the difference presented between how girls and boys learn,

process, and respond to information? Name two insights
you've gained:

1.
2.

What is the most important thing you learned about boy
brains?

What is the most important thing you learned about girl
brains?

How will understanding these differences help you relate to
your own teenager?

Considering the advice given on supporting your teenager
physically—eat healthy, get plenty of exercise, take
nutritional supplements, drink lots of water, get plenty of
rest—which ones do you find the most difficult to adhere
to yourself? Which will be hardest for your teen?

Teenagers are not fans of hypocrisy. What personal
changes are you willing to make today to model a healthier
lifestyle for your teen?

6

When There's More Along for the Ride

Normally, everyone was out of the house a little after seven, scattered throughout the area, to work and school. This morning, however, Mark lingered after breakfast, making a call on his cell phone and doing some work from the back office. He wanted to check something out; he wasn't exactly sure what it was, but something just wasn't right with Tiffany. He and Pam had talked about it a couple of nights ago but weren't able to come to any conclusions.

Mark found himself wishing that old refrain, "Why can't she be more like her sister?" He didn't want to feel that way but had to acknowledge he did, often. Sarah at this age had been so much more mature than Tiffany and tended to be more like him in personality. Tiffany was all over the map. He didn't know from one day to the next what—or whom—he'd have to deal with where Tiffany was concerned. Mark had trouble relating to her. She just never seemed to react well, even as a child. She was moody, often defiant, and, frankly, whiny. Nothing ever seemed to go right with her; everything was a problem. He shook his head and wondered, yet again, why she made living her life such a chore.

But this line of thought wasn't helping. It was stirring up his feelings of frustration and resentment regarding Tiffany, which didn't set well along with the worry threatening to coalesce. He could feel some sort of emotional storm brewing and was determined to pin it down early and get it fixed.

He was tired of all the things about Tiffany that needed to be "fixed." Sarah was happy and active, weathering her teenage years fairly smoothly. Andrew, thank heaven, was still in grade school, and—Mark had to admit he was thankful for it—he was a boy. Tiffany was his problem child. Shaking his head, he looked over at the clock. He just wanted to take a look at Tiffany before she left for the bus stop today; lately, it seemed she was doing her best to avoid him and her mother—well, the entire family, to be truthful.

Tiffany emerged from her room, ran quickly up the stairs and down the hallway to the garage, so preoccupied she didn't see him following her. As she reached up with her right hand to grab her jacket from the peg by the back door, Mark noticed something on the inside of her arm. It looked like a series of scratches, but they seemed too uniform. Startled to see him, she mumbled a generic good-bye, swiftly turned, and was out the back door before he had a chance to investigate further.

Puzzled, he wondered what could have caused those marks. They didn't have a cat. He hadn't seen them before, but maybe they were just something he'd missed. Mark decided to check with Pam about them that evening. It would be much better if she asked Tiffany; their relationship was marginally better than his and Tiffany's.

Pulling out of the driveway and heading to work, Mark flipped on the radio to his regular news station but wasn't really listening. Instead, he was thinking about Tiffany. What could have caused those marks? How long had she had them? Even though it was starting to get cooler with the onset of fall, he realized he couldn't remember the last time he'd seen her without a long-sleeved shirt on. He remembered over the summer at one point thinking it was odd that she'd wear shorts with a long-sleeved shirt but figured it had to do with some teenage-girl-wardrobe thing *so he hadn't really pursued it any further. Now, he started wondering again. Whatever those scratches were, Mark didn't think they looked right. Something was going on; he was determined to find out what.*

Dangerous Companions

Along the journey through adolescence, teens often allow dangerous companions. True, some of these companions are people—the flesh-and-bone, peer-group type—but others are behaviors that seem to attach themselves to a confused, overwhelmed, struggling-to-mature teenager. The more of these companions along for the ride with your teen, the harder that ride is going to be. In this chapter, we're going to look at these companions and help you learn to spot some things to watch out for.

Your teen may hold onto the identities of these companions as though they're a state secret. These are *his* friends; this is what *she* does. A huge barrier exists in the adolescent world between you and your teen where companions are concerned. Your teen will tend to view these things either as no big deal and none of your business, if benign, or as top secret, if not. Occasionally, you may have a teenager who will shove one of these companions in your face, as a way to punish, hurt, or push you away. Sometimes, a teenager will bring one of these to your attention, as a way to cry out for help.

Cut to the Quick

For Mark, the companion his daughter invited along with her on the road to adolescence was self-injury. This behavior is especially prevalent with younger teenage girls. Cutting has become a more widely known term for this pattern of self-harm or self-mutilation, but the behavior encompasses more than just cutting. Teens engaged in this behavior may use their own nails or a sharp object to scratch or gouge their skin. They may relentlessly pick at the scabs, reinjuring themselves. Some teens will burn themselves with cigarettes. Others will bite, hit, or bruise themselves. Teens have also been known to intentionally inflict pain by pulling out their hair.

Why would teenagers do this? As difficult as that question is to ask, the answer is harder to contemplate: Teenagers inflict and endure physical pain because they are trying to cover over, numb, or compensate for emotional pain. They exchange a pain that appears relentless and out of their control for a controllable pain. They exchange an inner one for an outer pain. By layering over and controlling the inner pain with the outer, the physical for the emotional, they experience a momentary sense of relief. This sense of relief from the emotional is real because the teen has bartered the release of those negative feelings for the physical act of self-harm.

As the relief is momentary and transient, however, it requires repetition; thus, some teens will turn cutting or self-injury into a ritual behavior. When under stress or overwhelmed with negative thoughts and feelings, these teens will set about to feel better. As they feel the physical pain or watch their own blood well to the surface and spill over, it's as if they are ridding themselves of their inner negative feelings. This is a coping mechanism, a strategy to feel better. It is strategy seized upon by some who have decided to isolate themselves from others and demand autonomy over their own solutions. It is, in other words, a behavior uniquely suited to teenagers who, in a flawed understanding of independence, decide they must be in control of their emerging selves, even their pain.

Though teenage girls cut and engage in self-injury at higher rates than teen boys, as a parent of either, you need to be aware of what to look for. Because the self-injury takes place on the physical body of your teen—a body your teen is loath to share with you in any way—you're going to need to be careful and alert.

Watch for unusual wounds. Mark's warning bells went off because the scratches on Tiffany's arm were too regular in appearance. Cigarette burns are distinctive because of their circular shape. All kids will knock into table edges and walls occasionally and produce bruising to the outer extremities, such as hands, toes, shins, outer thighs. Be alert to any wounds or bruising on inner, more protected parts of the body, such as along the inner arm, inner leg, or chest. Be aware of wounds that look suspicious or if the explanation you're getting from your teen just doesn't ring true.

Watch for repetitive wounds. Teens who engage in self-injury can choose a certain type of wounding or a specific area of the body to harm. A single scrape to an inner wrist is certainly possible, but if that same wound shows up over and over again, your teen could be engaged in ritual harming. The pattern to look for could be cutting, or it could include other kinds of injury. Watch for any sort of repetitious burns, as this could be a sign of "branding," which uses burns to cause the injury. Bruising to the same area of the body or with a pattern over weeks or months could be the physical manifestation of a teen's self-harming pattern.

Listen for unusual sounds. Teens can dissolve into a cocoon of self-absorption where reality somehow stops at their bedroom door. As such, they can sometimes forget that walls aren't impermeable and that sounds do carry. One of the self-harming behaviors is head banging. The harder they bang, the louder it gets. Depending upon the stealth of the teen involved, the area of the head used may not be visible; it could be the side or the back, which is covered by hair. Hearing head banging may be easier to detect than seeing it.

Watch for wounds that don't heal. Some teens will intentionally inflict a wound both for the initial injury as well as for the opportunity to continue that injury, picking at it just as it nears healing, in a cyclic manner. It can also be a constant picking—a failure to be able to leave wounds alone. You may be able to detect an absorbed fascination with picking at the wound. Be alert to pimples or acne and whether these heal or seem to constantly be disturbed.

Believe me, I understand this isn't anything you want to focus on as a parent. These aren't easy thoughts to consider. This kind of despair, driving a child to go to such lengths as self-harming, is terrible to contemplate. As terrible as the act of self-harming is, even more terrible, more painful, is the hurt that lies beneath the act. If you suspect your teen has begun to engage in any of these self-harming behaviors, you need to seek professional help with a trained health-care professional. The silver lining in all of this is your teen is actually trying to make him- or herself feel better. As misguided and self-absorbed a way as it is, your teen is trying to find a way out of and through the pain. As a parent, you can help him or her find a much better way.

Up in Smoke

It never ceases to amaze me how teens can look at adults and come to such upside-down conclusions. They are convinced that even though we're in our thirties, forties, or older, we somehow jumped right over being teenagers ourselves. When reminded of the immutable laws of time, they retreat into a rationale that says, "Okay, maybe you were my age once, but you don't know anything about what it's like to be *me*." It's as if adolescence is some sort of exclusive club they've just been let in to, and they can't imagine that you were ever part of that club at one time yourself.

Teens observe, presumably, their parents and other adults around them and perceive all of the privileges but overlook most of the responsibilities. Adulthood is all about the perks. They fail to realize, as teens, that they are still enormously supported by their parents or families, as they venture out onto the limb of adulthood. Most teens are still fed, clothed, housed, and loved, albeit by fallible, imperfect adults. While teens yearn to be left alone, we all know it can be an overwhelming thing to actually be alone and completely responsible for yourself.

Teens, longing to be adults on their own terms and misinterpreting the link between privilege and responsibility, can also emulate some of the very worst of adult behaviors. They sometimes look greedily on the negative aspects of adult behavior—like irresponsibility, aversion to commitment, or lack of integrity. Instead of seeing adulthood as a time for choosing what's right, they can instead see it as a time for choosing what's wrong. In this vein, teens have, for years, decided upon an odd rite of passage to prove their entrance into the circle of adults: smoking. Cigarettes are a symbol, a badge of rebellion. It seemed like, at least for a while, teens were getting the message, with fewer and fewer of them smoking. This declining trend, however, has recently slowed, according to a recent report from the Centers for Disease Control.[1] There is a stubborn status attached to smoking by some teenagers. It's even possible that the more a teen hears and reads about not smoking, the more attractive it becomes as a badge of independence and rebellion.

Teens can also smoke for all of the reasons adults do—as an appetite suppressant, as something to do to curb anxiety, as a calming technique. Just like adults, teens can become addicted to the nicotine in cigarettes very quickly. This nicotine can also be delivered through smokeless tobacco products like snuff, also called dip, or tobacco leaves, also called chew. There is even a trend now among teens to smoke tobacco through a water pipe or hookah, under the mistaken notion that this delivery system is less harmful. It's not, according to the National Institute on Drug Abuse for Teens.[2]

Again, we all know it; smoking is highly addictive. A rebellious, misplaced gesture to show independence as a teenager very often leads to a physical and psychological dependency as an adult. Smoking leeches health and life from your child. It's not a casual phase, one you can assume he or she will grow out of. If your teen has taken up smoking, you need to assist and support him or her to stop quickly and completely.

Check for the smell of cigarettes on clothing and hair. If your teen has his or her own car, check it for odor. Check bedrooms, bathrooms, garages for odor.

Watch for cigarette residue. Look for cigarette packs, not all of which are US made; teens have access to all kinds of cigarettes, including those produced in other countries, which can be brightly packaged and flavored. Look for cigarette butts, paper, smokeless tobacco pouches, or cans.

This is, obviously, going to be complicated if you smoke yourself. If you do, you know you need to quit. Perhaps you haven't been able to do it for yourself up to now, but can you do it for your teenager? Teens with parents who smoke are more likely to take up smoking themselves. Like it or not, where smoking is concerned, you are a role model and a motivator. For your health and the health of your teen, become motivated to quit.

The Mayo Clinic has put out "Teen Smoking: 10 Ways to Help Teens Stay Smoke-Free" as a guide for parents.[3] The number-three way for teens to stay smoke-free is for a parent either not to smoke at all or to quit smoking. Other suggestions include communicating your disapproval of smoking because, believe it or not, most teenagers care about what parents say. Talk candidly about the negatives to cigarette smoking or nicotine use. You can mention things like smelly clothes and hair, the way it stains teeth and gives you bad breath. There's always the health aspect of reducing lung function and causing you to wheeze and cough; it ages you prematurely. Of course, there's the money angle, as well. Tobacco products are expensive. This Mayo Clinic publication encourages you to do the math with your teenager, calculating the cost of an ongoing tobacco addiction. Teens have all sorts of things they want to spend money on—invariably more things than money itself. You and your teen may be astonished by how much money can go up in smoke with cigarettes and tobacco products.

Sticky Fingers

Jean was furious. It had already turned into an amazingly lousy day; the sun was shining, and she'd been called in at the last minute to work. All the stuff on her to-do list was shot, just like that. Oh, she could use the money—time and a half came in handy—but it was giving up one of her days off. So she hadn't been in the best of moods anyway, and then she got the call.

It was security at the mall, informing her that her son had been picked up for shoplifting. He was being held at the mall office, and police had been called. Perfect. She had to arrange to leave work three hours early, without really wanting to explain why. When she'd used "family emergency," her coworkers had reacted with misplaced concern. Thomas wasn't hurt; at least, *she thought darkly,* not yet.

She assumed the twenty-minute drive over to the mall would calm her down, but it was only making her madder. Shoplifting! Trying to walk out of that big-box electronic store with a lousy CD! He didn't even really listen to the CDs he had at home anymore; most of the music was downloaded to his iPod, which was permanently affixed to both ears. How much could it have cost? Fifteen bucks? If it was on sale, she was really going to blow a gasket.

This was just so humiliating. Everyone would think she was a bad mother. Everyone would think he was a bad kid. He wasn't; she wasn't. When she'd been called in to work, Thomas had asked if he could hang out at the mall with a couple of friends. She figured it would be better than staying home all day. It was a pipe dream to think he'd actually help out with anything on her list around the house, so she'd said yes. Jean had even given him ten dollars for lunch! He'd better have a darn good explanation for all of this, she decided as she pulled into the parking lot.

Walking up to the mall entrance, Jean felt like she was on auto-pilot. She walked through the glass doors but didn't really see them. What

possible reason could Thomas give for stealing from that store, even if it
was only a cheap CD? He probably wouldn't have a good reason. Maybe
his friends put him up to it, like a dare. Maybe he just saw it and wanted
it and didn't want to wait for his allowance, which he could just forget
about for the foreseeable future. Maybe he just did it without thinking.
How do you get a twelve-year-old boy to think things through? That's
what Jean had to worry about. All the store had to worry about was a
fifteen-dollar CD. She briefly wished she could trade places with the store
manager, as she headed down the nondescript hallway past the restrooms
to the office. The closer she got, the more she wished she was doing just
about anything else.

According to ShopLiftingPrevention.org, 25 percent of the $13 bil-
lion stolen from retail stores every year is done so by kids.[4] That's
around $3.25 billion from stores per year or almost $9 million per
day. That's a lot of fifteen-dollar CDs. The majority of shoplifters are
adult (75 percent), but of those, over half (55 percent) started out
shoplifting in their teens.[5] Some kids grab something once but are
so scared and ashamed they don't do it again. Others use it as a way
to get what they want without having to pay. Still others use it as a
way to demonstrate their independence and disdain for authority.
Whatever the reason, a lot of kids do it. According to the same set
of statistics, when asked, 66 percent of kids say they hang around
with kids who shoplift and 89 percent know of kids who do. In
all of this dreary information, perhaps the most disturbing piece is
"drug addicts, who have become addicted to shoplifting, describe
shoplifting as equally addicting as drugs."[6] That catches my attention
as a therapist. It should catch your attention as the parent of a teen.

Teens tend to steal things they want or things that give them status with their peers. If your teen starts wearing or possessing jewelry, clothing, or items you doubt he or she has the money for, start looking for things like receipts in wastebaskets or plastic merchandise bags. Anything purchased from a store is generally going to come with a receipt in the bag. If it's not in the house, check the car. If it's not in the car, ask. Stores are getting savvier about catching shoplifters, but the vast majority are never apprehended, and only half of those cases end up with police involvement.[7]

However, if your teenager is shoplifting but hasn't been caught, it doesn't mean there aren't consequences. Even a onetime incident of shoplifting can bring shame and a sense of failure to a teen. If it's more than one time, it could turn into a habit, an addiction that could stick around straight into adulthood.

Itching for a Fight

The more distressed your teen is over adolescence, the more susceptible he or she is to using anger as a counterweight to the felt burden of the teen years. Anger is a powerful emotion and an empowering physical reaction. To me, anger is *effective*. It effectively affects you—how you feel, what you think; it affects the parameters of any situation. Anger can propel you into flight or strengthen you for fight. In this state, you feel stronger, more alert, and more certain. As an adult, you recognize feeling stronger, more alert, and more certain isn't necessarily a good thing if you're headed in the wrong direction. Teens in an anger state couldn't care less about direction; they are just relieved to be headed somewhere, anywhere, other than where they were and to be feeling differently from how they were feeling. Anger is transformational; it takes you from one state of being into another. That other state of being can be a pretty heady place for a teenager.

Teen anger is generally expressed as irritation, annoyance, frustration, and lack of patience. She can't find her history book, which she's sure she left on the kitchen counter last night—but isn't there now. She confronts you and wants to know why you've moved her book that she needs *now* because she's running late. Startled by her intensity, you respond that you didn't see her history book, let alone touch it. Trying to be helpful, you suggest maybe she put it upstairs in her room. She counters with the fact that she's already looked *everywhere* upstairs and that it's nowhere to be found, implying by her tone, of course, that you are somehow to blame. Taking a deep breath, you ask if she's looked in her backpack by the front door. Without another word, she stalks off to the backpack, finds the book, and continues to exit out the front door without so much as a thank-you.

Teen anger can also be expressed through sarcastic and dismissive conversation. He informs you that he's headed over to a friend's house and that he's taking the car. You inquire why he hasn't checked with you first before making these plans because, after all, it is a school night, it's getting late, and, technically, it isn't his car. He further informs you that, yes, he knows what day of the week it is but that he still, technically, has forty-five minutes and he figured you wouldn't need the car anyway because you don't get out this late. All of this is said in a resigned, slightly bored tone, as if this were the one-hundred-and-tenth time he's had to explain it to you and the conclusion—that you should have no problem with this—is obvious.

Teen anger can also turn inward and result in a cloying shroud of self-loathing and criticism. She hates her hair, even though she just recently coaxed you out of a substantial chunk of change to get it styled. He never should have signed up for that advanced class because there's no way he's ever going to get the material and it's going to mess up his GPA and he should have known better in the first place than to try it because he's just not that smart.

All of these examples are fairly common, normal fits of teenager anger. They carry different names and flavors, but the underlying emotion is an anger reaction. But there is another type of teen anger that you need to watch out for. It's an anger that goes over the line from angst to aggression. It's the anger that expresses itself in rage. It is violent anger, deliberately hurtful. It is anger that finds its fulfillment in the hurt, humiliation, or domination of another person. This is anger meant to conquer, control, manipulate, and punish. It's dangerous and damaging to all parties involved.

This is anger that results in physical fights, intimidation, and bullying. It is powerful and can be very addictive. All teens—all adults, for that matter—get angry and do and say things they shouldn't. Those expressions of anger, however, should be accompanied by at least a twinge of remorse. Teens aren't always the best at expressing that remorse, but you should be able to detect it through actions, if not the actual words "I'm sorry." This other anger, though, is not regretted as much as it is reveled in. It is an anger that elevates the teen as he or she steps all over someone else. It isn't only physical intimidation; it is also manipulative, corrosive anger expressed through sarcasm and derision. This damaging anger feels good or, at least, feels better than the alternative. Stewing in this rage-filled, adrenaline high can move a teen back from the abyss of teenage dread—but at a dreadful cost.

Please be aware this type of anger may not be overtly directed toward you as a parent. It may be directed at peers, teachers, or other authority figures. This is anger that comes out as bullying, as intimidating others. This is "scorched earth" anger, an anger whose only objective is release, not resolution, restitution, or reconciliation. Because it is anger that cares little about consequences, it has the potential for great damage and needs to be addressed immediately by a health-care professional.

Tightly Wound

Teens have been described as tightly wound springs, kept at constant tension by their phase of life and physical development. Navigating adolescence is challenging, but some teens have a way of piling on additional pressures. On the one hand is the overachieving teenager who is determined to grab as much of life as possible in as short a time as possible. These teens have incredibly high expectations for themselves; they are perfectionists. Failure is not an option, and when failure happens, as it invariably does, it is greeted as a catastrophe. These teens have the type of schedule it takes a computer to calculate, plotted out to the minute, in order to shove in as many activities as possible. They gobble up responsibilities, tasks, and duties with abandon today, heedless to the overindulging consequences tomorrow. They cheat sleep, nutrition, relationships, peace and quiet, and a chance to recharge and reset. They are adolescent Energizer Bunnies; and, as long as they get juiced with whatever they can find or devise, they'll just keep going and going, doing and doing, until something breaks.

That's the worker teen. On the other side is the worrier teen. These are the teenagers who can't seem to finish anything. They worry about everything—whether it will be good enough, whether they should have tried it in the first place, what it will mean if they can't get it done. They constantly worry about girlfriends, boyfriends, the lack thereof, tests, how they look, what they wear, what other people think. They hesitate starting things or taking risks because they're worried about how it will turn out. You can't get them to make a decision to save their life. Even after a decision is made, it's constantly reevaluated and second-guessed.

The overriding theme for both of these types of teens is anxiety. The worker teen creates a life of anxiety by demanding an extraordinarily high level of personal achievement and perfect outcomes. The worrier teen creates a life of anxiety by doubting any level of personal achievement or even acceptable outcomes. This state of anxiety, whether manifested in the compulsion to go-go-go or in the hesitation to wait-wait-wait, can result in an anxiety disorder. The first is called *generalized anxiety disorder* (GAD) and is a state of being anxious all the time about nothing in particular. GAD is living life tightly wound. This isn't being worried about the test on Tuesday or what to wear to the dance on Saturday. Instead, this is waking up day after day with a sense of impending disaster, without really knowing why. It's just a sure feeling that something terribly wrong is going to happen and being worried about it, tense and alert. The symptoms of GAD include:

- Living in a state of constant worry, jumping from little thing to little thing, without any relief

- Trying to stop worrying but unable to
- Constantly on edge, wanting to relax but unable to
- Difficulty falling or staying asleep
- Feeling fatigued, sweaty, light headed, irritable, nauseated, out of breath, shaky, having trouble swallowing, getting headaches or bodyaches

GAD is a diagnosable and treatable disorder, determined by severity and duration of symptoms as well as impact on daily functioning. Overly anxious teens can be taught skills to combat persistent negative thoughts and coping strategies for mitigating worry and fear. This is a pattern of thinking or behaving that neither you nor your teen wants perpetuated into adulthood.

Sometimes, instead of anxiety casting a shrouded pale over all aspects of your teen's life, it will instead attack and attach itself to a single moment of absolute dread and terror. This is called a panic attack, where your teen will become convinced something terribly wrong, even fatal, is happening physically. It can be perceived as having a heart attack, with pounding heart, sweating, weakness, dizziness, or fainting. A panic attack's physical symptoms accompany an overwhelming sense of unreality and a fear of losing control. Usually, panic attacks are over in around ten minutes, but the psychological impacts last much longer. Teens who undergo a panic attack may suddenly avoid any activity they perceive as a precipitating event. It may develop into a fear of going to sleep, as panic attacks can occur at night. After the attack is over, the fear of a reoccurrence takes center stage. According to a publication on anxiety disorders by the National Institute of Mental Health,

"Panic attacks often begin late in adolescence or early adulthood but not everyone who experiences panic attacks will develop panic disorder."[8] If your teenager complains of any of these physical symptoms clustered together, you need to rule out a physical cause. If a physical cause cannot be determined, don't become complacent or think your teen is "just imagining" the symptoms. They are real and need to be addressed. Your first stop is your physician, but it shouldn't end there if there is no physical cause found or if these panic episodes continue to persist. Look for a professional therapist or counselor to support your teen.

Food for Thought

Over the years, I have worked with so many teens in the area of eating disorders. It is generally in these adolescent years that the seeds of an eating disorder take root and grow to strangle the joy of childhood and choke out the promise of emerging adulthood. Eating disorders manifest themselves through food, but food is merely the mechanism for the pain that lies beneath. It is not surprising that adolescence and eating disorders go together because this is the time of life when teens are making their own decisions. They are breaking away and are trying out control over their lives. One of the things they find they can control is what, when, and how much to eat. If they don't want to eat, they won't. If they do want to eat, they'll find a way. They'll also find a way around what they have or haven't eaten. Food is also an instant gratifier. If you don't eat, you feel it; if you do eat, you feel it. When so much of a teen's life revolves around waiting and hoping and maybe and might be, food is concrete. As such, it can become an alluring strategy for coping with life.

Anorexia is, simply put, self-starvation. It is the willful restriction of caloric and fluid intake in order to lose weight beyond what is healthy into the unhealthy, dangerous, and even fatal. It is a compulsion to restrict, beyond all reason and logic. Anorexics are not reasonable in their eating. They develop highly elaborate rituals and rationales for what they do, often based not on science or fact but on their own misunderstandings, biases, or desires. I've worked with anorexics who thought calories could move from one food product to another, simply by being in proximity to each other—a bizarre sort of cross contamination. Others would eat only a very small list of foods, deeming all others unsafe for consumption. This sort of black-and-white reasoning finds a suitable breeding ground in the black-and-white world of adolescence. It is a time where a little bit of knowledge can be dangerous because a little bit becomes all that is required to justify an unreasonable action. What is desired is not knowledge but proof that their line of thinking is right, that they are right, because being right means being in control.

Bulimia is, in some ways, the opposite of the self-starvation of anorexia. Bulimia is the overconsumption of calories and the subsequent purging of those calories, either through self-induced vomiting, use of laxatives, or excessive exercise. Bulimia is using food to provide comfort and relief. In some ways, it is not unlike self-injury, which uses a physical pain to numb a psychic one. Bulimia takes another physical experience—eating—and uses it to fill a psychological void. Once the relief is experienced, the fear sets in; the panic ensues. All that food cannot be allowed to digest and become fat, so all that food must be purged, the damage undone, the evidence flushed.

Food is meant as nutrition, not as a way to deal with life's challenges and stresses. It is meant to fuel the body, not numb the mind.
Food is not a drug, but that is how it is used in an eating disorder, as
a mood-altering substance. Teens need to learn how to acknowledge
their moods and work through them. This is part of the process of
maturing. Any activity that short-circuits this maturation is detri-
mental to their development into adulthood.

Back when we went over smoking, I said it would be difficult
to deal with your kids about cigarettes if you smoked yourself. I
would venture to guess that more parents are going to have even
greater challenges in this section where food is concerned because
the use of food as "drug of choice" is so prevalent in our culture.
You don't need to be anorexic or bulimic to use food as companion,
comfort, distraction, reward, punishment. If your teen has issues
with food, you may need to accept that he or she has learned some
of that behavior from watching you. Teens watch you and make
judgments on your veracity about all sorts of things based upon
what they see. They listen to what you say, but they also very much
watch what you do. (If you are concerned your teenager has developed an eating disorder, I urge you to read my book *Hope, Help,
and Healing for Eating Disorders*. There is information on this book,
and others I've written, in the back of the book.)

Not Old Enough to Drink

According to information from the CDC, 42 percent of high school
students have used alcohol.[9] Almost a quarter of high school students
say they have episodes of heavy or binge drinking. That's a lot of
teenagers engaging in alcohol use, all of it underage and illegal. But

teens don't necessarily use what is legal to determine what to do; in their minds, they are old enough to drink when they decide to do so. Our teens are deciding when it's okay for them to drink 42 percent of the time. Because of this high number, you as a parent need to be aware of if and how your teen is using alcohol.

I'd like you to be honest with yourself here and really evaluate how you think about alcohol. I've been surprised by how many parents will rant and rave against their teen's drug use but have no problem with that same sixteen-year-old having a beer after mowing the lawn on Saturday or joining in with the adults for a glass of wine at a family get-together. Alcohol is a drug, even if it is legal for adults to consume, and more teens use it than tobacco or illicit drugs.[10] So ask yourself, how do you feel about alcohol? Do you use it? Do you allow your teen to use it? Do you use it responsibly, or do you have to admit you go over the line sometimes?

Again, this is important because how you feel about alcohol filters down to your teen. Teens have underdeveloped off switches, which makes even casual alcohol consumption a recipe for real disaster. Just picture an inebriated teen behind the wheel of a car, or in a crowd of hostile peers, or in front of a darkened storefront, or with an equally inebriated and sexually aroused boyfriend or girlfriend, or exposed to a variety of illicit drug choices, or attending a job interview, or sitting down for an important test. I think you can see where I'm going with these visuals. None of those situations is going to be made better or safer for your teen if he or she has been drinking.

Depending upon how you feel about drinking, you may never actually see evidence of your teen's alcohol use. If you've allowed your

teen to consume small amounts of alcohol at home, you'll probably never see how much more and often he or she is using alcohol
away from you. If you're absolutely opposed to it, your teen will
take his or her drinking elsewhere and you won't see it, but you can
still look for signs of it. Watch for the smell and the effects, such as
slurred speech and loss of coordination. If you are concerned, obtain
a chemical-dependency assessment or evaluation for your teenager
from a trained professional.

Yes, alcohol is readily available to teenagers from unscrupulous
sources, but why would they go to the trouble to try to obtain it
elsewhere when they can just get it from you? If you have alcohol
around your home, I urge you to keep close track of it and even have
it under lock and key. You cannot know all of the physical and psychological triggers for alcohol abuse and dependency that may reside
within your teen. Don't take the chance. As much as it depends on
you, keep your teen safe and away from alcohol.

Drugs

Alcohol is a drug, but it obviously isn't the only one out there you
need to be worried about. There are a plethora, and they can be
found anywhere from a weed-infested, dirty alleyway to the polished
and pristine environment of your own medicine cabinet. The greatest danger where drug abuse and your teen is concerned is thinking
it couldn't happen to you or your teen. It can; it does. Go up to
your teen's middle or high school sometime and just watch as all of
them leave for the day. According to the CDC, one in five is using
marijuana.[11] They may have smoked that day or be heading to smoke
as they walk past your car.

This is the reality for your teen; it's pretty much everywhere and available. In addition to marijuana, teens have access to cocaine, heroin, ecstasy, methamphetamines, hallucinogens, inhalants—you name it. And that's just what's available today; who knows what people will come up with for tomorrow?

Teens are also raiding their parents' and grandparents' medicine cabinets for a cornucopia of prescribed pharmaceuticals, including antidepressants, pain medications, and sedatives. You need to accept that your teen is under assault by a dominant culture that screams for a pill every time something goes wrong—wrong as determined by self—and from a subculture that's only too happy to get your teen's money regardless of what happens next.

Once your teen descends into the drug culture, it's a tough, long, hard-fought battle to get him or her back up and out. That culture does not surrender its victims easily, constantly grabbing and snatching and snaring them back down again. Rescuing your teen can become the literal fight of your life. I've known many parents who have exhausted just about everything they had to do it. Would they do it again? Absolutely, but the cost is immense on all sorts of fronts—emotional, relational, physical, spiritual, financial. I've known families that sacrificed much and won. I've also known families that sacrificed much and still lost. When drugs are involved, it is life or death; please don't delude yourself to the contrary.

Truth or Consequences

There is so much riding on your teen's successful journey into adulthood and so much that can come along for the ride, unwanted and dangerous:

- Self-injury
- Tobacco/nicotine addiction
- Shoplifting
- Violence/aggression
- Anxiety
- Eating disorders
- Alcohol abuse/dependency
- Illicit/prescription drug use

Believe me, I understand how overwhelming all this can be. I can understand that a part of you wants to reject even thinking about any of these in conjunction with your child, but denial is not a luxury you or your teen can afford right now. You need to know and recognize these as dangers facing your family so you can be alert and prepared to take action to intervene.

In the next chapter we will look at teenage depression. All of the behaviors in this chapter can be companions to depression, and a long-term pattern of any of these behaviors can lead to depression. They are circular in nature because all of these behaviors point to and lead to an overwhelming sense of despair and hopelessness in teenagers. These are what to watch for. These are what you should be evaluating and holding up to the light, peering as best as you can through your teen's behaviors, to determine if a pattern or a problem exists. This evaluation process is ongoing, by the way, and will continue at the very least until your teen graduates from high school and, more likely, for several years beyond that. You're not off the hook when that eighteenth birthday happens or that diploma is in hand.

Bringing It Home

This is the chapter on co-occurring issues—the unwelcome and dangerous companions that can hitch themselves to your teenager's ride through adolescence: self-injury, smoking, shoplifting or stealing, anger and violence, stress and anxiety, eating disorders, alcohol and drug use.

I'd like you to think over that list and evaluate your attitudes about each and what's happening with your teen through the following questions:

How do you feel about each one? Do you see each as harmful to your teen? If not, why not?

Did you engage in any of these behaviors when you were a teenager?

Which one do you find the most dangerous to your teen? Why?

Which one are you the most willing to overlook? Why?

Which one would make you the most uncomfortable to talk about with your teen?

What has your teen heard from you about each one? What have you said to him or her?

How has that message been supported or undermined by your actions?

What could you do differently to match your actions with your words? How likely are you to actually do that? Why?

If you feel uncomfortable or unable to talk to your teen about any one of these behaviors, is there someone else you can ask, someone your teenager trusts and will talk to?

What concrete actions could you take today to help protect your teen from any of the dangers on that list?

What are you willing to change about yourself to help your teen?

For that last question, you may need to get out the photo collage you created in chapter 1. It doesn't get any easier to change behavior as adults than it was as a teenager. If you are still engaged in any of these destructive behaviors, you haven't found the motivation yet to stop even though you know how damaging they are. Look over the pictures; what is it going to take for you to change?

7

When the Ride Goes Off Track

She couldn't care less about anything; it's as if, in an attempt to conceal everything about herself, she covers up even what interests her. In order to stay anonymous, she seems to work so hard at giving nothing of herself away. With her apathetic attitude, she's hiding in plain sight. It didn't used to be that way, but it definitely is now.

He's missed another three days of school with vague complaints about not feeling well. First it's his stomach; then it's a headache. The only thing that seems to help is to shut himself up in his room. He doesn't want to eat anything; he doesn't want to do anything but listen to his iPod or be on the computer all night, which he must be since it's impossible to wake him up in the morning.

She seems to have only two prominent emotions: anger and despair. When confronted about her anger, she just shuts down and says it doesn't really matter anyway. She's started making sarcastic, under-her-breath comments that are really scaring you. When you ask her to repeat them, she just shrugs, says, "Never mind," and walks away.

He's doing something; you know it, but you can't put your finger on it. You keep saying you're going to start searching his room, if he's ever out of it, which he rarely is. He doesn't hang around with his friends anymore, and when he does go out, it's to meet kids whose names you don't know. A half a dozen times you've stood at the doorway to his room, trying to decide whether to cross over that threshold; you haven't yet.

Everything is a big deal to her these days. Everything is a catastrophe, a disaster. Any little thing that happens mushrooms into a huge crisis, with you either squarely in the way or squarely to blame. She's always been a little dramatic, but that behavior has just gone off the proverbial deep end. It feels like she's drowning in her own tears and she's dragging you under with her.

He used to proudly show you his progress reports and report card. Now, it's nearly impossible to get any intelligible response about his grades, which are in a steady, if not swift, decline. You know; you've gone online. When pinned down, he's come up with a variety of excuses, none of which really seem to ring true. You're worried because these grades count, putting future college plans in jeopardy, to say nothing of the future itself.

She's dropped at least fifteen pounds in the last several months. At first you were pleased, thinking she was finally dropping the last of her baby fat, but now you're worried. She absolutely refuses to discuss it with you. Family meals have become either all-out war zones when it's just the family or silent no-fly zones when others are present. The more you express your concern, the more weight she seems willing to lose.

It's like his mind is made out of Teflon—nothing sticks. You can tell him a million times to do something, but when you confront him about it, he looks like a deer in the headlights, befuddled by your frustration. You feel like you've been transported back in time to when he was a toddler and you needed to speak clearly and slowly, making sure his eyes were on you. This, of course, doesn't really go over well now. But you're at a loss to explain this inability to focus. Is it just you he's tuning out, or everything?

You could swear you smelled alcohol on her breath the other night when she came in, but she went upstairs so quickly to get ready for bed, you weren't sure. By the time she came back down to wish you a good night, which, come to think of it, was kind of strange in itself, she'd taken a shower and brushed her teeth. The only things you smelled then were her usual shampoo and the mint toothpaste. By that time, it was too late, and you just let it go.

You can see it in his face, which is strange because usually his face is devoid of any emotion. That's the problem—where is he? Where has he gone to? What is he thinking about? If he's in trouble, why doesn't he come to you for help? When did you become some sort of enemy, to be kept oh so carefully at arm's length? You've done nothing but love him his entire life. When did that become not enough?

Catching Smoke

As we've seen in previous chapters, dealing with a teenager can be a dicey proposition in the best of times. On any roller coaster, part of the ride is taking that occasional plunge, but what happens when the drop becomes too steep or the ride veers off track? As a parent, your tolerance for a rough ride may be different from your teen's. So how do you know if your teen is having a bad day or a bad week or something more? How do you know if the withdrawal and slump in grades are normal or something to worry about? How do you know if it's just teen angst or something worse? How do you know if your teen is just unhappy because of a breakup or doing poorly on a test or if this unhappiness has spread to life in general?

How do you know what you're dealing with when your teen has become adept at avoidance? He's quite capable of figuring out and telling you what you want to hear so you and your disquiet will quietly go away. She has the ability to block any genuine concern with a concussive and shrill blast of anger. Getting to the bottom of a problem you merely suspect and your teen barely understands is like catching smoke and trying to examine it in your hand. As tempting as it may be to give up the whole proposition of trying to catch smoke in the first place, there is the unsettling reality that where there's smoke, there is often fire. This fire has a name: It's called depression.

Kids get depressed, just like adults. It's something, as a parent, you need to be aware of and look out for. A depressed teen does not have the wherewithal, generally, to come to you for help, especially when one of the symptoms is isolation. If you're waiting for your teen to come to you, you're going to be waiting a long time, maybe too long. So you need to be proactive. Know the signs. Even though all kids are different, there are some specific things to look for, according to the National Institutes of Health's National Youth Violence Prevention Resource Center (that's quite a mouthful, but, luckily, the website is a bit shorter—SafeYouth.gov). No one of these signs is a definitive red flag that says, "Yes, your teen is depressed." Rather, they form a pattern of concern. They should catch your attention and slow you down long enough to investigate the source of the smoke, even if you have trouble catching it in your hand.

So what are these red flags that parents need to watch for, if they are wondering if their teen is teetering on the edge of something more serious than teenage angst? I have listed them below, and following the list is a more detailed explanation of each:

- Negative feelings or behaviors lasting more than two weeks

- Loss of enjoyment in established activities
- Restlessness, fatigue, or a lack of motivation in school
- Marked increase in irritability or impatience
- Feelings of being weighed down
- Loss of physical and emotional energy
- Marked changes in appetite or weight
- Lapse in personal hygiene.
- Social isolation from family or friends
- Taking up with a new set of friends
- Impulsive thinking or rash judgments
- Inability to make decisions, concentrate, or focus
- Marked increase in frustration or anger
- Feelings of sadness and worthlessness
- Expressing feelings of stress and inability to cope
- Ongoing complaints of headaches, stomach-aches, bodyaches
- Marked change in sleep patterns
- Avoidance of added privileges

Negative feelings or behaviors lasting more than two weeks. She doesn't make the school play. He breaks up with his girlfriend. She gets chewed out at work. He tanks a test at school. All kids are going to get knocked down by life. Life happens, and sometimes it isn't pleasant to deal with. Teens are more susceptible to "the slings and arrows of outrageous fortune" than adults because they have less experiential history under their belts and just aren't done developing. They haven't learned yet that life goes on and that failure isn't the end of the world. For a teenager, with their laser focus on themselves and their own issues, failure does seem like the end of the world. They have more of the passion and less of the perspective. So they can get knocked down easily. What you want to watch for is how long it takes them to pop back up. Days are normal; even a couple of weeks are normal; months are not. If your teen still hasn't regained some natural emotional buoyancy after two weeks, pay attention.

Loss of enjoyment in established activities. This one can be tricky to diagnose because teens are notorious for changing their minds. Someone they loved and couldn't live without two days ago is now a person they can't stand to be around. They may suddenly take up an interest in the latest social cause because of a movie they saw. Because so much of the world is ahead of them, they will often pick and choose, seemingly at random. However, if your teen has always enjoyed playing sports but, now, seems completely disinterested in physical activity of any kind, pay attention. If your teen flips off an activity switch, look to see if that activity is being replaced by another. It's perfectly reasonable for teens to decide they're tired of playing soccer and decide instead they enjoy theater or music. If your teen turns off a favored activity and does not replace it with anything but apathy and lethargy, pay attention.

Restlessness, fatigue, or a lack of motivation in school. This often plays out in a student missing school, whether you are aware of it initially or not. In Washington State, we have a law called the Becca Bill, which mandates that schools track both absences and tardies. It also mandates parental involvement with the court system if a child is either late to school or absent from school too often. Parents here are made aware when their teen is checking out of school physically.

What may not be as evident is when a teen is showing up physically but is checked out in every other way. Grades slip, but parents aren't always made aware of problems until a midterm exam or at end-of-semester grades. If your teen avoids going to school or his or her academic performance across a broad spectrum of subjects steadily declines, pay attention.

Marked increase in irritability or impatience. This one can be difficult to track because teens live in a state of impatience. Tomorrow seems like a week from now. A week from now seems like a month. A month seems like a year. Hours can seem like forever. However, by adolescence teens should know and understand the concept of delayed gratification. They may not like it, but they should be able to have a level of perspective on what it means to wait. The thing to look for here is excessive irritability turning to outright anger or hostility. If your teen, instead of being mad at "the world" or the way things are, focuses this anger toward you or others, pay attention.

Feelings of being weighed down. Sometimes teens will interpret feelings of depression as a metaphoric weight. This weight will sap their moods, interfere with physical activities, and envelop them in a feeling of being burdened. Often, teens internalize the pressures they feel at this age—pressures to fit in socially, to mature physically, to advance academically, and to achieve peer expectations. This pressure produces feelings of anxiety, which can add to the perception of being physically out of whack. If your teen talks about things like feeling pressured, never having enough time to get things done, or always feeling stressed out about life, pay attention.

Loss of physical and emotional energy. This sign goes hand in hand with the previous one. The constant pressure a teenager feels can lead to a numbing out, with a corresponding loss of physical energy and motivation, as well as an emotionally flat persona. It's as if your teen decides it's just too hard to hold up under the pressure and, consequently, physically and emotionally checks out of life. This can be difficult to detect if your teen rarely stops long enough to give you the time of day. It's important for you to determine to stay aware of your teen's general demeanor. There is a difference between your teen being too busy to slow down and talk to you and being intentionally distant and unmotivated. When a teen begins to adopt a "who cares?" attitude about life, pay attention.

Marked changes in appetite or weight. When life becomes too stressful for teens, they will often reveal the stress they're under by either a rapid weight increase or a rapid weight decrease. For some teens, food becomes self-medicating—a way to feel better, even if temporarily—whether it is consuming the food or restricting it. Never known for good nutrition, a teen's food choices may take a sharp dive downhill, with caffeine, sweets, and junk food the preferred choices. On the opposite spectrum, a teen may react to the increased feelings of stress and despair by a severe loss of appetite. The grayness with which the world appears translates into a loss of interest in food. The "who cares?" attitude about life becomes a "why bother?" attitude about eating. If your teen suddenly puts on or takes off significant amounts of weight when there is no medical reason, pay attention.

Lapse in personal hygiene. Some teens couldn't care less about how they look—or, at least, that's the impression they wish to convey. Since time immemorial, teens have specifically undertaken clothing and hairstyles designed to produce a startled reaction in parents and other adults. A spiked red Mohawk is an intentional style choice. Chains and piercings are intentional fashion preferences. Teens usually spend a great deal of time preparing their "casual" look. But what I'm talking about here is a lack of care about personal appearance, a sudden, marked neglect of hygiene. If your teen stops caring about looks or even cleanliness, pay attention.

Social isolation from family or friends. All teens go through times when they really don't want to be bothered by other members of the family. Occasionally, they'll kind of hibernate away from friends, if they're working through something and need some alone time. However, teens are generally social creatures and need the interaction with other people to help validate their feelings of self-worth. Teens tend to run in packs; just take a look at any major mall or movie theater on a Friday or Saturday night. When depression starts to leech all enjoyment out of life, one of the things to go is socializing with friends. If your teen suddenly decides the confines of his or her room is room enough for weeks on end, pay attention.

Taking up with a new set of friends. Sometimes a depressed teen will withdraw from established friends and family. But, still needing social interaction and validation, he or she will begin to draw in new friends. These new friends may be markedly different from the old ones. They may be more "shadow" friends; you'll hear their names but never seem to actually meet them. If you do, they may appear suspicious, indifferent, or even hostile to you. If your teen has begun to use drugs or alcohol to self-medicate a depressive state, he or she will tend to acquire friends or acquaintances with similar habits. If your teen starts taking up with friends you've never met or who are rude or defiant, pay attention.

Impulsive thinking or rash judgments. It is the nature of teenagers to leap before they look. The part of their brains that screams, *"Caution!"* where appropriate is still a couple of years away from full development. They exist within a shell of invincibility and don't always appreciate the natural consequences of their actions. However, impulsive as teenagers are, they generally have reasons for why they do things. Those reasons may not always be thought out to the degree we, as adults, would like, but teens generally have given their actions some thought. What to watch for here are rash, impulsive decisions or actions, without a solid basis or because of a negative basis. This negative basis could be based on a sense of despair, something like, "It doesn't matter anyway," or based upon an anger reaction. If your teen begins a pattern of sudden, impulsive decisions, without being able to articulate why or with negative reasoning, pay attention.

Inability to make decisions, concentrate, or focus. This sign is akin to the previous one and is sort of the inverse. Instead of making rash, impulsive decisions, your teen now can't seem to make decisions at all, even insignificant ones. He or she can't remember simple instructions or complete a task. These teens can appear distracted and disoriented. It's as if their brains are engaged in some sort of mental spinning that drowns out what you want them to hear and keeps them from staying at one thing too long. I know some of you are protesting that your kid is like that even on good days! That can be very true, but the component you want to watch for is a despair, frustration, or anger at this behavior from your teen. If your teen becomes agitated and confused when asked to concentrate or make a decision, pay attention.

Marked increase in frustration or anger. A certain level of distress is part and parcel of the teen phase. The sheer uncomfortableness of adolescence is a cause for reasonable frustration and anger. It's why teens are often given a "get out of jail free" card by many parents for their occasionally hostile behavior. They can tend to be human powder kegs, just waiting for the right circumstances to set them off. Parents can be aware of their volatility and make adjustments. But what if your teen begins to be angry at everything? What if fighting and yelling and put-downs become a pattern? If your teen appears wound up tighter than a spring, just waiting to unload at any provocation, pay attention.

Feelings of sadness and worthlessness. Some kids will react to their depression through feelings of rage, spewing out vitriol and violence on those around them. Other kids will retreat into themselves, exhibiting a profound demeanor of sadness and despair. They may spend time crying or talking to themselves in a negative way. Personalizing the problems they perceive in their world, they may begin to engage in self-blame, determining life has no hope because they are hopeless. If your teen appears wrapped in a cocoon of sadness, pay attention.

Expressing feelings of stress and inability to cope. As adults, we tend to dramatize our own experiences as being especially difficult or challenging. Each of us has probably used some sort of variation of the "walked a mile in the snow to school" routine where our kids are concerned. We think they couldn't possibly have it as rough as we did. Because of this, we may be blinded to some very real stresses our kids undergo. This is especially true if our kids are taking a different path through school and adolescence than we did. If we were average students in school, we may not realize the pressures even an academically gifted child can feel. If we didn't really date until we were in college, we may not recognize how painful adolescent romantic relationships can be. Our kids are different from us and will, therefore, experience stresses that are different than ours were, along with all of the "normal" stresses of the teenage years. If your teen verbalizes feelings of constantly being overwhelmed, this isn't a time to discuss how he or she couldn't possibly have it as bad as you did at that age. It's not a time to compare and minimize; it's a time to pay attention.

Ongoing complaints of headaches, stomachaches, bodyaches. For some teenagers, the emotional pain they feel comes out as physical pain. They may not pinpoint emotional distress but will complain of headaches or bodyaches. These can be ongoing without any definitive physical cause. They're interpreting not feeling right with not feeling well. As such, they may combine these complaints with a reduction in activities and increased isolation. They don't feel good so they don't feel good enough to do much. If your teen expresses a constant litany of vague physical complaints, pay attention.

Marked change in sleep patterns. Teens are notorious for weird sleep. They can stay up until two in the morning, cramming for a test, and then sleep fourteen hours straight on a Saturday. With burgeoning independence brings more evening activities, while school still starts really, really early. They shortchange themselves on sleep during the week and spend a good deal of the weekend comatose— or at least it feels that way to you as no amount of vacuuming, door slamming, or laundry noise appears to rouse them before the afternoon. Given this already erratic sleep pattern, it can be difficult to detect when something shifts. However, if your teen begins to spend considerably more time sleeping or appears to have a problem relaxing and staying asleep, it's time to pay attention.

Avoidance of added privileges. One of the things teens seem to crave more than anything is added privileges. They're not always so keen on the responsibilities that go along with them, but anything that equates to more "freedom" in their life is generally seen as a good thing. For a depressed teenager, however, added privileges are a burden because he or she doesn't feel able to cope with life as it is. A normal teen chomps at the bit to get out and get going; a depressed teen appears resigned to staying put, staying isolated, staying invisible. If your teen seems reluctant to ask for or rejects the added privileges of getting older, pay attention.

Smoke Detector

Over and over again, at the end of each heading in the above section, I put the admonition in to "pay attention." That should be your official role as the parent of a teen. I understand it's a lot, but someone has to do it and that someone has to be you. You not only need to watch for and be aware of the normal roller-coaster ride of adolescence you and your teen are on, but also need to be alert for problems that can veer that ride off track. You are now in the smoke-catching business, or, to put it another way, you are your family's smoke detector.

Have you ever burned the bread toasting in the oven or failed to open enough windows when cooking on the kitchen grill? Sure enough, that annoying loud scream of the smoke detector will go off, causing general upset and ear discomfort. In a rush, you dive to open as many windows as you can, along with the front door, in order to just make the stupid thing shut up. That's going to be you for a while—the annoyingly vital yet irritating thing your teen wishes would just shut up. At least, he or she will seem to want that on the surface, but don't take offense; you're just doing your job. Your job is to pay attention for smoke and alert people when it's time to investigate and make changes. It might even be your job to alert your teen and the rest of your family to more than smoke—to a real fire. In the chaos and pain that follow, you might even feel to blame because you're the one who sounded the alarm. Take heart; no one ever went back into a burned house and busted up the smoke detector that saved the lives of his or her family. I promise you, it will be worth it. You may just need to wait awhile to hear "thank you."

So go ahead and be like a fly on the ceiling—or like a smoke detector on the ceiling—quietly monitoring the situation in your house and in your teen, ready to raise an alarm when conditions warrant. The conditions talked about in this chapter and others you'll read about need to be monitored.

Bringing It Home

Just as you did in the last chapter, I'd like you to go over these teenage conditions as a sort of checklist, to determine if any are starting to produce smoke in your teen's life. I warn you, these may be harder for you to get through because few things cause a stronger fear reaction in a parent than thinking about his or her child in some sort of distress or danger. If you're feeling this way, remember that each one of these conditions is a reason for concern but certainly not panic. You may have a teenager who is feeling completely overwhelmed because she's simply trying to do too much. A frank, realistic discussion of what all these activities mean to her, to you, and to the family may be all that's needed to help put some perspective on the situation. You may have a teenager who has developed a habit of staying up all night on the weekends and sleeping all day as a way to avoid dealing with a difficult sibling or to be able to play a favorite game without interference. A frank, realistic discussion of family expectations, along with really listening to what's going on, may be all that's needed to reestablish a more normal—at least for teens—sleep schedule. Your job is to detect the smoke, not fan the flame of any given situation into a full-blown catastrophe. Be alert; be wise; be real as you consider what role these conditions may play in the life of your teenager.

Put a check next to the conditions below that describe your teen:

O Negative feelings or behaviors lasting more than two weeks

O Loss of enjoyment in established activities

O Restlessness, fatigue, or a lack of motivation in school

O Marked increase in irritability or impatience

O Feelings of being weighed down

O Loss of physical and emotional energy

O Marked changes in appetite or weight

O Lapse in personal hygiene

O Social isolation from family or friends

O Taking up with a new set of friends

O Impulsive thinking or rash judgments

O Inability to make decisions, concentrate, or focus

O Marked increase in frustration or anger

O Feelings of sadness and worthlessness

O Expressing feelings of stress and inability to cope

O Ongoing complaints of headaches, stomachaches, bodyaches

O Marked change in sleep patterns

O Avoidance of added privileges

As you did in chapter 2, I'd like you now to go back over your list and give some sort of time range for each of these that you marked. How long has this been going on?

Think also about the pattern to each behavior. Have you noticed an increase or a decrease in the severity or frequency? Go back and put either an upward arrow if it's increasing, a downward arrow if you find it decreasing, or a flat line if it's seems to be fairly consistent.

Do several of these conditions tend to run together? Do you notice an increase in feelings of sadness or worthlessness when there is more social isolation? Are there fewer complaints of bodyaches when there is a more normal sleep pattern? Be aware of these conditions individually, but also consider how some of them may be linked together with your teen.

Now, I'd like you to think about the top concerns you have. What worries you the most? Why is that? Is it something you can relate to from your own adolescence? Can you determine what seems to distress your teen the most out of any on this list? What you determine to address first may not be what your teen would identify. As much as possible, follow your teen's lead on what is the most problematic.

Finally, I'd like you to go back over the checklist you did in chapter 2. Read over what you wrote, and think about that checklist in light of this one. As you look over those behaviors and characteristics and what you wrote about each, including time range, are there any that affect or add to the conditions you've identified here? Sometimes the difference between the two checklists is one of degree. They can be very similar, and it can be confusing separating out what is just teen behavior and what has become a breeding condition for depression. Look for how severe the behavior is, how long the behavior has gone on, and how debilitating the behavior is to normal life functioning.

Teens can *get* depressed without *being* depressed. But even getting depressed is a challenge in their lives where you can offer guidance and support. You should not make it a goal to "fix" your child or take over whatever difficulty he or she is going through. One of the main benefits of adolescence is learning how to begin to handle adult-sized life challenges while still supported by caring adults. If you remove all of their obstacles, they will fail to develop their adult-needed muscles and will constantly be looking backward, as a child, to you to save them. Instead of looking backward, their eyes should be firmly forward, toward their future as adults.

8

When It's Time to Get Help

Robert was at a loss. He knew the divorce was an end to his marriage with Beth, but he hadn't planned on the damage it had done to his relationship with Brianna. So many things had changed all at once—finally telling the kids about the divorce, him moving out and having to sell the house, Beth taking on another job, and Brianna starting high school. He'd done his best to partner with Beth to try to mitigate what was happening to the kids, but, truthfully, they hadn't been that successful. It was just so hard to think ahead where the kids were concerned when he had to be concerned about himself. After all, this was just anguish for him.

But things had settled down and had been going relatively smoothly for the past several months. The kids seemed to adjust to the artificial every-Wednesday, every-other-weekend thing that just drove him crazy on the one hand but for which he was honestly grateful on the other. He and Beth were at least talking to each other without arguing, which was why he was at a loss. If he started up the conversation he just felt he should in his gut, Beth was bound to take it badly.

Robert felt Brianna was having some real problems. She didn't seem to want to do anything she used to anymore. He couldn't even get a response to going shopping or heading out to the park to run his new dog. Brianna had always loved dogs, and she'd barely even acknowledged when he'd gotten Charlie. Maybe she was mad it was a boy dog instead of a girl dog—he had no idea—but Charlie was cute and cuddly and full of energy, and Brianna appeared like she couldn't care less. Something was wrong.

He also didn't like how Brianna looked. She'd dropped a lot of weight since the divorce and didn't have any interest in eating much whenever she was at his house. At first, he'd thought that it was just puberty kicking in and that she was finally shedding some of her baby fat, but this was getting disturbing. Every time she showed up now, thinner than she was the week before it seemed, it was like an indictment of him, of his choices and the upheaval in her life.

She refused to talk to him or even interact with her younger sister, who made the changes so much more apparent with all of her ten-year-old enthusiasm. Brianna had always been quieter, more serious than Kayla anyway. Now the differences were huge and impossible to ignore. If he kept on ignoring Brianna's weight issue, maybe it would get better on its own. If he mentioned it to Beth, she could take it that he was saying she wasn't being a good mother, or, even worse, she'd blame him for the changes. It was a risk, but, deep down, he couldn't shake the feeling that Brianna was somehow at risk. How long should he let it go on? What was he supposed to do?

If she was mad at him and was mouthy or disrespectful, it would almost be better. At least then they'd have some sort of communication. It was the quiet that just unnerved him. She was quiet when she arrived, whether she went up to her "other" room or sat in a corner of the living room. She was quiet during meals, even though he'd banned all electronic devices at the table. She was quiet whenever forced to participate in the family outings that tended to be planned on his weekends. She was quiet when she walked out the front door, back to her mom. Too quiet, like an eerie calm before a storm.

Teens live amid such tumultuous waters, it can be hard to detect if something is just an adolescent squall or if there's a real storm brewing. As a parent, you're caught between a rock and a hard place. You don't want to be perceived as a meddling parent. You want your teenager to learn how to handle adversity on his or her own, without always wanting you to step in and save the day. You've gotten the message of "hands off" loud and clear when it comes to your teenager, but you know something's not right. You've waited and you've watched, and that feeling in your gut just won't go away. You feel like you ought to do something, but you don't know what.

When to Get Help

In the last chapter, I talked about parents needing to be like smoke detectors, ever alert and vigilant in case of fire. Unlike battery-operated smoke detectors, you're not equipped to know the exact particulate level that presents a danger in your teen's life and start beeping your head off. This isn't a mechanical switch; it's a judgment call, and that's where parents can have problems. Step in too soon, and you look like a hysterical parent, further alienating your kids. Step in too late, and, well, the consequences of that can be ghastly.

Complicating all of this is your teenager's uncanny ability to hide how he or she is really feeling and doing. Living in an adult world, teens become quite adept at telling adults what they think we want to hear. With all of the other stuff we've got going on in our lives, we're often just as willing to believe and not question what they say. Teens live within a shell of protective coloration, meant to shield their inner selves from others—especially, perversely, parents.

Sometimes, it isn't evident that a storm's brewing until your family is lashed in the ninety-mile-an-hour winds caused by an eating disorder, substance abuse, early pregnancy, or self-harm. These are high stakes so, as a parent, I'd rather look ridiculous and be considered as overreacting than be wrong and left wondering why I didn't do something sooner.

One of the biggest red flags that you need to be aware of in teenagers, as we discussed in the last chapter, is clinical depression. Again, we're not talking here about normal, periodic, short-term bouts of teen angst. Instead, we're talking about a long-term pattern of despair, despondency, and lethargy. A couple of down days with teenagers are a normal consequence of the age; it takes them awhile to process their feelings—in some cases to even connect with their feelings. During that sorting-out period, a teen's emotional equilibrium can get a little skewed. Multiple weeks and, certainly, months, are not healthy or normal.

For adolescents, these feelings of despair are truly overwhelming. The unique thing about teens is they can be feeling this way and do their very best never to show it. Of course, complete concealment isn't possible so they may lapse their camouflage in front of friends or in unguarded moments when they think no one else is paying attention to them. It can also come out in sarcastic, caustic, or fatalistic statements about themselves, the future, and life in general.

The more of these indicators that exist in a teen's life, the heavier the burden that teen carries. These can build up over time, brick by brick, until your teen's attitude about self and life collapses. When this collapse occurs and your teenager enters a severe depressive episode, the warning signs will become more pro-nounced and harder to hide. The lethargy and "who cares?" attitude will take center stage even more, along with increased references to hopelessness, helplessness, and even death. That inner dialogue of hopelessness can leak its way into comments that are anything but casual.

Even if your teenager is not forthcoming about how he or she is doing or feeling, you can collect collateral information. One of the first things to be aware of is what challenges your teen is currently facing. Normally resilient, steady adolescents can be knocked over by significant traumas or stresses in life. They have fewer experiences with which to marshal a response, and their brains are still working out how to integrate upper-level reasoning and long-term strategies. Using a flood analogy: A teen barely treading water can be forced under by waves you've dismissed as small and insignificant. If teens are caught in a trough of lowered self-esteem, having a fight with a friend (romantic or not), tanking a test, failing an audition, or being laid off a part-time job can dunk them under. You need to watch to see how soon and how well they're bobbing back up. When you know what your kids are doing, you can watch, listen, and make yourself available.

As we talk about when it's time to get help for your teenager, I'd like to add a couple of gender-specific behaviors here. In order to interrupt or relieve feelings of hopelessness, teenage boys can resort to risky, thrill-seeking behavior—from stupid stunts to illegal activi-ties to anger and fighting. These more demonstrative behaviors can hide a significant feeling of despair and depression in a teenage boy. The very bravado required is an attempt to hurdle over the feelings that threaten to bring him down. For girls, the thrill-seeking behavior can have more to do with relationships. In order to seek relief from inner turmoil, teenage girls may enter into sexually charged, physically accelerated relationships.

As a parent, you may be shocked and focused on *what* they've done instead of understanding and dealing with *why* they've done it. And I will readily acknowledge that in a crisis, you've got to deal with the what first. But once the panic has faded, it's very tempting to crawl back into a hole and refuse to take the time, effort, or energy to uncover the why. Pretending everything will just go back to normal, as if nothing ever happened, is just one more form of adult hypocrisy that enrages and alienates teenagers. The "normal" that you so desperately want to go back to was killing your teenager, figuratively. By trying to recapture something that didn't really exist, you tell your teenager that your comfort is more important than his or her life. This is not a message you want to convey to a confused, troubled, hurting adolescent.

Again, it really comes down to a judgment call, but there are some specific situations that require immediate action by you as the parent and the adult. You may want to go back and review the earlier chapter on co-occurring conditions again. I've listed them here, also, as a reminder:

- Self-injury, such as cutting or burning
- Tobacco/nicotine addiction
- Shoplifting/stealing
- Violence/aggression
- Anxiety

- Eating disorders
- Alcohol abuse/dependency
- Illicit/prescription drug use

These are cause for a full-blown fire alert. You need to get help for your teen immediately, no matter how much resistance you encounter. Allow me to add a few more that have long-term consequences and need to be immediately addressed:

- *Pregnancy*—This applies whether your teen is the mother or the father. As a Christian and as a father, I believe in the inherent value of life from the moment of conception. Creating another human being is one of the most consequential acts a person will ever make. There are vast emotional, relational, and spiritual consequences that need to be addressed. It changes everything, whether or not that life is carried to fruition. Your teenager will need immediate guidance and support.
- *Bullying*—Teenagers have the capacity for almost surgical cruelty. Teens are tied to peer pressure and acceptance, so those same peers can know exactly where to place the blow to do the most harm. With technology, the venues for injury have expanded, as well as the range of the humiliation and attack. If your teenager is being bullied, you need to take action to protect your child by putting a stop to

the behavior. This is not how people should treat each other. Self-worth, boundaries, and courage are invaluable adult characteristics. If your teenager is bullying others, you also need to take action to protect your child by putting a stop to the behavior. Again, this is not how people should treat each other. Compassion, empathy, and sympathy are invaluable adult characteristics.

- *Academic difficulties*—Your teenager has another, primary identity: student. It's not just about reading, writing, and arithmetic; this is the age of learning how to learn. Not all kids handle this "assignment" well. There are a variety of conditions that can interrupt and interfere with your teenager finding success academically. I'm not talking here about becoming the class valedictorian or acing the SATs. Rather, I'm talking about experiencing the normal, graduated progression of learning that allows for your teen to reach academic markers of comprehension, retention, and application. This isn't just about getting into a college or technical school; how teenagers do academically is integrated into how well they do—or don't—think of themselves. In so many ways, school is a competition—something teenagers respond to. It is a way they judge others and themselves. If your teenager is struggling academically, he or she is struggling personally; you cannot separate the two.

The Cost of Help

Once you're ready to pull the switch, to set off the alarm and admit that your teenager needs more help than you can provide, there are a variety of resources available to you. However, I have to caution you that these resources are not always easy or pleasant to access, and almost everything you do for your teenager is going to take more time than you thought, be more work than you thought, and cost more than you thought. You've got to be prepared to be patient, persistent, and realistic. You've also got to be willing to adapt to the emerging information and be ready to respond. You've got to be willing to love your teenager even when that teenager starts gobbling up an inordinate amount of your time, energy—both physical and emotional—and money. Difficulties are called that for a reason—they are hard to deal with and require energy of all kinds to overcome.

Getting help will mean exposure, letting other people into your life, your family, especially the parts you are least willing to share. It also means allowing in other opinions, information, and expertise. You will generally be the one paying the bills, but you will not have all of the control. Depending upon the state you live in, teenagers have rights outside of their parents regarding medical, mental-health, and substance-abuse services, including what information these professionals are legally allowed to share with you.

I say all of this not to discourage you but to prepare you so you'll have realistic expectations. You must be willing to do what it takes to get your teenager the right help, in the right place, with the right person. Getting help can be a hit-or-miss proposition. It can be difficult to figure out just what the real issues are, and then, once you've done that, it can be difficult to find the right person or service that can truly help. You'll need to guard yourself against the inevitable discouragement that happens when it's a miss. Sometimes it's a miss because the person or place just isn't the right fit, and sometimes it's a miss because your teenager just isn't ready to respond and accept the help. There's a coordination that needs to happen, and sometimes it takes several tries to be successful.

You'll also need to guard yourself against the resentment you'll feel toward your reticent, reluctant teenager. In your mind, you're trying your hardest to save this kid's life, and all you're getting in return are a lousy attitude, nonexistent gratitude, and begrudging cooperation. Remember, your teenager is confronting his or her worst adolescent nightmare—not being able to handle life when it really counts. Troubled teens, already despondent, will feel like even more of a failure when the facade is ripped down and the truth of what they've been trying desperately to hide is revealed. Unless you're remarkably fortunate, you're going to have to wait for a while for the hugs and thank-yous and "I love yous" to surface.

The full-blown blast of anger you get often arises out of the depth of your teenager's fear—remember that. I don't think I've seen an angry teenager who didn't experience deep-seated fear; fear of being unlovable and unloved; fear of failure and the humiliation of not living up to expectations; fear of the future; fear of being unable to live life on his or her own; fear of inadequacy; fear of risk; fear of pain. Getting help for your teenager is not usually a smooth path.

It's rocky and bumpy, and you've got to be determined to walk it, no matter what, for the sake of your teen.

Have you noticed that, in this section about the cost of getting help, I haven't talked much about money? People and services cost money, but getting help for your teenager is going to cost you more than that. It's going to cost you time, energy, patience, strength. It's going to cost you love; you will need to expend the love you have for your teen in order to get the needed help. You're going to need to love your teenager more than you do your comfort or your time or your perceptions. You're going to need to love your teenager more, even, than you do your own weaknesses; getting help for your teen has a way of uncovering your weaknesses and requiring you to change for the good of your teen.

And, yes, getting help generally means spending money. I'm not going to get into dollar amounts here, but you're going to need to accept that not all of the help available for you and your teenager will come without a monetary cost to you. There are school resources, community resources, and religious resources that can be accessed for no or reduced cost, but it is not realistic to expect that all the help needed will be without financial impact. You need to determine what you're able to do and how much you're able to contribute financially. If you have insurance coverage, call your carrier and ask specific, detailed questions regarding exclusions, deductibles, and coinsurance. You're going to need to count the cost. Over the years, it's been very difficult to watch families start into something like counseling only to decide, right when the teenager was beginning to make progress, that it was too expensive and stop. You need, as a parent, to decide what that help is worth and what you value as a priority and make decisions accordingly. And please remember, your teenager is watching and evaluating your choices.

Where to Get Help
Primary Care Physician

It used to be that the first line of defense for parents was the family physician, who knew the child, knew the parents, and was able to provide helpful, thoughtful advice. That just isn't the kind of world most of us live in anymore. We're more transient so we tend to move around and switch doctors. More people don't even have a family doctor anymore, choosing to go to storefront walk-in clinics and rely on school physicals. Time to really talk has been replaced by technology and assistants and minutes-long visits with the physician who has a quota of so many patients per hour.

All of this discourages the type of relationship and trust preferred to seek out help for your teenager. If you don't have a regular pediatrician or physician for your teenager, can I please suggest that you do so? This professional is your partner in safeguarding the health of your teenager. Every teenager should get a thorough physical at least once a year. There's a lot going on in that body of theirs, and teens are notorious for pushing the envelope and not bothering to really take care of themselves. Also, they're not always predisposed to listen to you. It's good to have someone else in your corner, supporting your messages about healthy eating, exercise, and proper sleep. Your teen's physician can also test for, diagnose, and treat physical conditions that can cause depressive symptoms, such as hormonal imbalances, anemia, or attention-deficit/hyperactivity disorder, to name a very few. This is a time of massive change in the body of your teen. You need a caring, knowledgeable physician in your teenager's corner, to help provide you with information and action.

School System

By the time teens get to high school, parental involvement in the schools has dried to a slow trickle compared to the level of commitment (room parent, parent meetings, birthday parties, student-teacher conferences, school fund-raisers) during grade school years. The last thing teens want is their parents to show up at school, on their turf, reminding all of their peers they actually have a family instead of existing as a self-contained, quasi-adult unit. While adults have a work-face and a family-face, teens tend to have a school-face and a family-face. It's just too weird to try to accomplish both at the same time so most teens would rather keep school and parents separated and at a safe distance. This is a hurdle you're going to need to jump in order to seek out help for your teenager in his or her academic world.

Because of societal changes, schools are becoming more than just places of learning. They also exist as a conduit for information about family services and community resources. This is true at the school level and also true at the school-district level. There are school- and district-level counselors who can provide insight and help to parents. For the most part, these professionals are caring and passionate about their work and your kids. They are also, for the most part, really, really busy because of the number of kids they have charge over. This is true for teachers at the high school level as well. My experience is for either of them—teachers or counselors—you have to be proactive; you need to call them and set up a time to come and talk about what's happening with your teenager. Teachers are often the first level of entry into what help is available through the school district. Next are school-level counselors and then district-level counselors and psychologists. Of course, teenagers find the adults they trust to talk to, whether a past or present teacher, a custodian, a counselor, or a coach.

These resources are available not just because your teen is getting a D in Geometry. A teenager who is having difficulty at home can also be having difficulty at school, even if that difficulty isn't necessarily academic. Many of the problems that threaten to pull teenagers under have to do with how they are relating to their peers. Schools are peer-relationship incubators. They are where teenagers spend a good portion of their time connecting. Because of this, schoolteachers and administrators have become over the years somewhat expert at spotting and understanding what's going on with the teens in their schools. They also see those teens wearing their school-face, a face you may or may not see as a parent. Seeing that face can help them give you needed perspective on what is going on with your teen and where to get help.

Ideally, schools and parents should be in partnership with each other, but, sometimes, it can seem like a competition. Parents get the idea that teachers don't think they do enough or don't welcome them into the arena of professional academics. Teachers get the idea that parents expect them to fix their kid with some sort of educational magic wand. Parents think teachers and the schools should do more; teachers and the schools think parents should do more. So sometimes, both groups spend too much energy blaming each other and not enough just trying to figure out what to do to help the teen. As far as it depends upon you, try to remove blame and an adversarial nature when dealing with your teenager's school, whether at the school or district level. Find people and ways to form partnerships. And make sure to remember to listen to your teenager. You're going to get information and insight from teachers and school staff, but you're also going to get opinion and, sometimes, bias. Work to integrate what you know about your teen, about your family, about your situation with what you're being told by others. As you're looking for people to listen to for help in understanding what's going on with your teenager, don't forget to listen to your teenager.

When accessing school resources, please realize you need to go through a hierarchy and a procedure. These generally start at the classroom level, progressing to the school level, with the district level being last. Be patient, and allow yourself to take the time to go through the steps. These are people you want to understand you, your situation, and your desire to find help for your teenager. They have, however, a chain of command they need to follow and procedures in place in order to access graduated resources. You, as the parent, are an independent agent. They, as district employees, are part of a system. That system has resources you should be able to access to help your child, but they are the gatekeepers of those resources. You can't go around them; they need to open the door.

Private Resources

You may decide to seek private resources to obtain help for your teenager. These are generally the resources that come with a financial consideration. As a parent, you are able to retain counseling services for your teenager, although, as I said before, states have different age parameters for when a parent can compel a teenager into counseling.

If you determine to seek counseling for your teenager, be prepared with a list of questions you'd like answered, as a way to screen out the choices available. You may need to make initial choices based upon your insurance coverage. If so, I encourage you to contact your insurance carrier to determine what your potential benefits are under your policy. Many people assume that mental-health or chemical-dependency benefits are the same as medical benefits, with the same limits and co-pays, but this is not necessarily so. Know ahead of time what benefits your teenager has under his or her coverage for all three—medical, mental health, and chemical dependency. Depending upon the situation, your teenager may need to access all three to get the help needed.

Some parents have expressed a fear of exposure even calling their insurance carrier to ask about different benefits, as if calling on Monday means an all-staff memo at their work site about it on Tuesday. Private health-care information is legally protected and must be kept confidential. Whether at the school-system level or through private providers, your teenager and your family have legally mandated confidentiality on these kinds of matters. Don't allow your unrealistic fear of exposure to present a barrier to getting the counseling your teenager needs.

What Does Counseling Look Like?

Over the years, I have seen the cultural stigma regarding seeking counseling ebb somewhat, but it still exists in some parts of society and among some people. People who will readily go to a surgeon to set a broken bone will shy away from going to a counselor to set a broken heart. If their car needs a tune-up, they go to a mechanic, but they won't go to a counselor if their career or their life needs a tune-up. They'll go to a chiropractor to get a spinal adjustment but won't go to a counselor to get an attitude adjustment. Counselors are professionals, trained to help people accomplish their goals. My goal—and the motto of my counseling practice—is helping people change their lives for good. Counseling isn't a denigrating experience; it's an empowering one. And it can be especially empowering for a troubled teenager.

The first visit, usually, is just for the counselor to determine what the issues are, as reported by the teenager. What is going on? What would the teenager like to have happen? From there, the counselor, along with the teenager, comes up with a plan on how to accomplish the goals. Along the way, the counselor will often obtain permission from the teen to be able to speak to parents, other adults, school counselors, or physicians to help define the issues and facilitate appropriate strategies to achieve the goals.

This can be a difficult time for parents. Parents can be anxious about what the teenager is telling the counselor—is it the truth? Is it everything the counselor should know? What is my teenager saying about me? Whose side is the counselor going to be on? Because of this, if at all possible, it's a good idea for the parent to be receiving some counseling as well, with an eventual eye toward doing joint family counseling. Think of teenagers as a family weather vane; they can tend to highlight family difficulties and personal issues. If that becomes your situation, consider now as the time to do the work toward recovery yourself. There's nothing that says both you and your teenager can't work in tandem on life, personal, and relational healing.

Generally, the type of therapy your teen will engage in is called cognitive-behavioral therapy. Cognitive-behavioral therapy is a two-pronged approach. The first part, the cognitive, deals with the mind and helping your teenager come to an understanding of what the truth is about a given situation, circumstance, or behavior—where it comes from and what the true issues are. The second part, the behavioral, recognizes that while knowledge is good, it's only truly effective when it's coupled with positive action. Your teen must understand what the issues are, and then he or she must understand and integrate the actions necessary to effect change.

Some people have called this "talk therapy" because it's essentially a journey to discovery through verbalizing thoughts and reasons. A professional therapist is trained to know what sorts of questions to ask to guide the discovery process and what sorts of actions to suggest to encourage the implementation process. It is not, usually, a one- or two-visit proposition, especially not with teenagers, who require more time and effort to win over and establish a relationship with. This isn't like having a boil lanced. You're not stitching together a finger; you're stitching together a relationship. That takes more time so you'll need to be patient. Usually, after the first several visits, the counselor will give recommendations for how long to schedule out appointments.

Be prepared to try a couple of counselors. Your teenager is not going to open up to someone he or she doesn't feel a connection with. Teenagers can be maddeningly opaque about who they're going to click with; it's kind of like deciding without him what sort of shirt he'd like or picking out for her what shoes she'll wear—only more difficult. Ideally, to help with the bonding, it's good to find a counselor who has already demonstrated an ability to connect with other teen-agers. This isn't a guarantee the counselor will do the same with yours, but it's a good place to start. And it isn't always about age; teenagers often choose people of very different stages of life to connect to, like teachers and grandparents. This connection isn't something you can orchestrate; you have to allow it to happen organically with your teenager. If the first person doesn't work, talk to your teenager about why—not as a way of judging but as a way of understanding—and take those insights into account as you try someone else. You can ask questions about the person's background, including work with teens; general counseling philosophy; and willingness to integrate faith into the counseling in order to feel comfortable about whom to present to your teenager—but your teen will make the final determination as to whether this person is the right one.

Once your teen has found someone he or she feels comfortable working with, the best way you can help is with consistency. Make attending appointments a priority. The next thing you can do is give your teenager some space. The first thing you say to your teen after a counseling session shouldn't be, "So what did you talk about?" Teens need privacy and processing time.

If your counselor suggests additional testing or services, make sure you understand what is being suggested and why. This isn't any different from medical testing, in that the terminology can be confusing and, frankly, scary at times. Since we counselors do this all the time, we may find it hard to remember that not everyone is familiar with our tools or our terms. It's okay for you to make sure you understand what's going to happen before it does. Your anxiety will not be positive for your teenager; ask enough questions so you understand and can convey your calm and understanding to your teen. And again, if you're using private insurance, make sure to contact your carrier and ask about the testing; some companies cover it, and others don't.

What about Antidepressants?

Whether or not to prescribe antidepressant medication for clinically depressed teenagers is undergoing a serious societal discussion. On the one hand are those who say that putting a teenager on an antidepressant actually increases his or her risk of suicide. On the other side are those who say that untreated depression can also increase a teenager's risk of suicide. This is truly a damned-if-you-do-and-damned-if-you-don't type of argument.

It is true that research has led the Food and Drug Administration (FDA) to issue advisories regarding adolescent antidepressant use, including warning individuals, families, and health-care professionals to closely monitor anyone under twenty-five taking antidepressants for increased signs of suicide, both during the beginning of treatment (which was defined as the first one to two months) and any time there is a dosage change.[1] The medications this warning applies to include the following:

Anafranil (clomipramine)
Asendin (amoxapine)
Aventyl (nortriptyline)
Celexa (citalopram hydrobromide)
Cymbalta (duloxetine)
Desyrel (trazodone HCl)

Effexor (venlafaxine HCl)

Elavil (amitriptyline)

Emsam (selegiline)

Etrafon (perphenazine/amitriptyline)

fluvoxamine maleate

Lexapro (escitalopram oxalate)

Limbitrol (chlordiazepoxide/amitriptyline)

Ludiomil (maprotiline)

Marplan (isocarboxazid)

Nardil (phenelzine sulfate)

nefazodone HCl

Norpramin (desipramine HCl)

Pamelor (nortriptyline)

Parnate (tranylcypromine sulfate)

Paxil (paroxetine HCl)

Pexeva (paroxetine mesylate)

Prozac (fluoxetine HCl)

Remeron (mirtazapine)

Sarafem (fluoxetine HCl)

Seroquel (quetiapine)

Sinequan (doxepin)

Surmontil (trimipramine)

Symbyax (olanzapine/fluoxetine)

Tofranil (imipramine)

Tofranil-PM (imipramine pamoate)

Triavil (perphenazine/amitriptyline)

Vivactil (protriptyline)

Wellbutrin (bupropion HCl)

Zoloft (sertraline HCl)

Zyban (bupropion HCl)[2]

The literature also includes explicit instructions that if your teen is currently taking an antidepressant, you should not discontinue that usage without consulting the prescribing physician.

These warnings present a dilemma to parents who are used to turning to a doctor for a pill or prescription to handle issues. The government does not put out warnings like this lightly, so it is definitely something to be taken into consideration. So what do you do if your teenager's primary care physician or a psychiatrist wants to put him or her on an antidepressant and you're just not willing to take the risk? Please be aware that in some states, the decision about whether to start an antidepressant may not legally be up to you. You may be legally obligated to pay for it, but your teenager, especially an older teen, may be the one to say yes or no. In Washington State, the age of consent is fourteen years old.

However, as the parent, you have a decision to make with your teenager. Even if state law says you make the call, your teenager still has to cooperate and actually take any medication as prescribed. If you can't get him to eat his broccoli or her to wash her contacts, how are you going to ensure your teen is taking the medication when and how he or she should, especially when that teen is out of your sight for hours on end? These medications tend to take weeks, if not months, to start to show effect—and only if taken as prescribed. The whole thing could be a huge exercise in futility if your teenager is not on board. As the parent, you need to be on board, as well. The decision on whether to take an antidepressant should be made in conjunction with your teen and the physician. Use needs to be monitored by all three of you to make sure any antidepressants prescribed are working and effective.

Before you and your teenager make a decision regarding antidepressants, I would encourage you to consider seeking out the professional advice of a naturopathic physician. We utilize the services of naturopathic doctors in my treatment facility because of our focus on the whole person and desire to integrate homeopathic and nutritional strategies whenever possible. These naturopathic physicians do the same sort of physical exams, blood work, and medical testing. And when warranted, they can and do prescribe pharmaceutical medications, including antidepressants. However, this is not the only tool available to them, and they will often prescribe common-sense, practical changes in diet and lifestyle, along with targeted nutritional support, to counter symptoms of depression.

Adolescents are young and, therefore, physically resilient. When cognitive-behavioral therapy is combined with a return to a healthy, nutritious diet, targeted nutritional supplementation, exercise, and strategies for achieving adequate and effective sleep, kids can bounce back. All of the stresses that cause adult bodies to break down also take a toll on teenagers, no matter how invincible they consider themselves. But, once those stresses are addressed and reduced, it's remarkable how well teenagers can respond to treatment.

Antidepressants for teenagers, in my opinion, should only be used after:

- The teen undergoes a thorough physical examination, including blood work.

- Ongoing counseling has not produced the desired results. However, counseling should still continue, along with the medication use.
- Lifestyle changes, such as an intentional effort to engage in healthy, nutritious eating and regular, condition-appropriate exercise, have not produced the desired results. Again, these efforts should continue, even with medication use.
- Targeted, physician-directed, nutritional support has not produced the desired results. Any antidepressant usage should be coordinated with the physician prescribing the nutritional support, to avoid negative interactions.
- The severity of the depressive condition medically necessitates use, after consultation with mental-health and medical personnel.

Once an antidepressant has been prescribed, I believe it should be the lowest effective dose for the shortest time possible. In the interim, the above strategies can still be implemented; however, again, any nutritional supplements should be evaluated with the specific antidepressant in mind, in order to avoid interactions.

Antidepressants should not be a long-term solution for most teenagers. In most cases, there are other strategies to consider and try before antidepressants are chosen. Because antidepressants are so readily available, they are often prescribed. However, they are not always the best or most effective solution in the long run for your teenager. This is a decision you and your teenager want to consider and research before you decide. As you monitor the situation, remain in communication with your teen and his or her prescribing physician. There are certainly times and circumstances where antidepressants are effective and create improvement. The goal, however, should be to reduce the amount taken and, as soon as medically appropriate, discontinue use.

Make a Decision

It's amazing how quickly time can flash by, especially when you're trying to make a decision. Denial and resistance are so strong, especially in parents when it comes to our kids. We so desperately want the uncomplicated, the safe, even the status quo, it can be as hard to pry us from our current state as it is to move a boulder with a straw. We don't really want to move because moving means acknowledging the awful truth that something is wrong—and not just wrong with us, wrong with our child, who, though a teenager, is still a child to us.

It's also hard to get that boulder of denial and wishful thinking to move because moving means heading down a slope when we have no real idea how long it goes and what, exactly, awaits us at the bottom. So it's denial of what we suspect we know, wishful thinking to stay with what we'd rather know, and outright fear of what we don't know. We're also terrified of making the wrong decision. That's a lot of motivation to just stay put, paralyzed, and hope and pray things will get better on their own.

If your teenager needs help and you do nothing, you may be lucky and your teen may find his or her own solution without you. Of course, teenagers aren't known for understanding and factoring in things like long-term consequences of actions.

Their short-term solution could end up causing even longer-term issues. You may be lucky, and some other adult in your teen's life will notice and take action in his or her behalf. Of course, teenagers, having even greater freedom and ability to form independent connections with others, just might end up diminishing or severing connection with you.

If you can see that your teenager is engaged in a battle for happiness or academic success or sobriety or relationship or is just plain in over his or her head with life, it's time to act. Enter the field and partner with your teenager to come up with solutions, resources, and help wherever possible. Even if your teenager initially refuses to engage to protect him or herself, stay with it. Keep presenting solutions, resources, and help. If you leave the battle, teens have much less chance of winning it on their own.

Create a Support Team for Your Teen

At The Center, the health-care facility I founded almost thirty years ago, we utilize a team approach to recovery, with mental-health counselors, chemical-dependency counselors, physicians, and dietitians. Together we coordinate professional efforts for the benefit of those who come to work with us. I'd like to suggest that you consider creating such a support team for your teenager. It's important that the professionals assisting your teenager are aware of each other. Teachers and school counselors need to be aware if your teenager is engaged in chemical-dependency treatment. Physicians need to know if your teenager is seeing a counselor, and certainly the reverse is true. The recovery of your teenager should remain the center of attention, with those involved coordinating and cooperating, instead of focusing just on individual areas of expertise.

As you're gathering this team, be sure to include other adults as appropriate—for example, coaches and extended family, such as aunts, uncles, and grandparents. Talk to your teenager about who should know and to what level. There is confidentiality, and then there are secrets. Confidentiality is meant to protect, but secrets can damage and lead to shame.

Finally, be sure about your own attitude regarding your teenager and getting the help needed. As the adult, you need to be sure you're not burdening your teenager with an extra load of guilt and shame yourself. Again, it's like the broken-arm analogy—if your teenager broke an arm, you'd go to a doctor. You wouldn't put it off or complain out loud about the cost or berate your teenager for not having stronger bones. No, you'd take immediate action and get your teenager the care necessary. Getting the kind of help talked about in this chapter is the same thing—only without the bones. But, even without the bones, don't delude yourself into thinking that the pain isn't as real or the damage as consequential.

Needing help is painful, but so is getting help. It's painful in that it requires time and energy and coordination and resources and money. Getting help requires recognition that help is needed and patience to do what is necessary to get that help. Getting help means an end to denial, an acceptance of the way things are, and hope for the way you want things to be. Needing help changes your life, but so does getting help—not always in ways you want, as it requires giving up a portion of control over the situation into the hands of others. You need to be willing to stay the course once you start on it.

Bringing It Home

You've spent a great deal of time up to this point evaluating your teenager. Have you identified areas where your teenager needs more help than you can provide? If so, you need to come up with a plan to address those needs.

- Identify the area where your teenager is struggling.
- Determine possible people and places to go to for help.
- Communicate your concern with your teenager.
- Together, agree on a first step to take toward getting help.
- Together, identify an alternate step in case the first doesn't work.
- Together, come up with quantifiable goals and outcomes that will mean success.
- Reassure your teen of your love, acceptance, and support.
- Continue to work toward achieving the goals, even if it becomes difficult, including resistance from your teenager.

If you have multiple areas where you believe help is needed, begin with the one that is generating the most negative impact in your teen's life.

9

Crisis of Belief

Judy kept looking at the clock, wondering how close Jeremy was going to cut it to curfew. For sixteen-year-old Jeremy, curfew was midnight on a Saturday, though moving it to the a.m. hours had been a long, hard-fought battle. The only way she'd given in to a time she continued to consider too late was because Jeremy had promised he would still be up and ready for church on Sunday. The closer he cut it to midnight, though, the harder it was for him to get up in the morning. Even when he did get up, he wasn't the most pleasant person to be around, especially when she was trying to prepare herself spiritually to worship. Less-than-loving thoughts tended to invade her mind when she had to deal with a grumpy, grouchy, resistant teenager.

Regardless of how difficult it was, Judy determined they were all going to go to church as a family. It was what she did growing up, and it was what she wanted for her family. Church was important. Jeremy might not appreciate it now, but Judy was sure he would later. She didn't know how she'd have survived young adulthood without God in her life. That's when all of it had become real to her—when God had intervened and rescued her, more times than she could keep count. Judy believed, and she wanted Jeremy to believe, as well.

Sometimes, she questioned herself. Should she continue forcing him to go to church, or did that imply that having him go through the motions was good enough? Should she allow him to decide for himself and let his faith and desire to come be authentic? It was 11:52 at night, Bob was *already asleep, and she found herself going over the argument again. No, she wasn't going to let him decide because she was afraid of how often he'd decide not to go. Plus, Bob had already weighed in with his opinion on the subject—his house, his food, his rules; everyone goes to church.*

More than anything, Judy wanted to see signs that Jeremy was coming closer to a decision for God himself. She didn't want to pressure him into anything more than Sunday-morning church attendance, afraid she'd drive him away. Afraid if she did; afraid if she didn't. Without answers, Judy did what she normally did; she prayed. She prayed and watched the clock turn over to 11:59.

Up to this point, we have been focusing primarily on the physical, relational, and sexual changes occurring during adolescence. Another major change is that teens are coming into their own spiritually. For Christian parents, this spiritual emergence is an added source of joy and anxiety. It's an added layer of anticipation and expectation. Everything else has here-and-now consequences, but spirituality, faith, and belief have hereafter consequences. Christian parents worry not only about how their kids are going to do in this world, but also about how they're going to fare in the next. Complicating this, of course, is that teens can be even more tight lipped about how they're feeling spiritually than how they're feeling sexually. Some parents decide it's just too hard to have The Sex Talk with their kids, so they leave it up to teachers and the middle-school health curriculum. Some parents find it just too hard to have The God Talk with their kids, so they leave it up to ministers and youth pastors. Your kids need to know and hear about sex from you, and they need to know and hear about God from you.

In some ways, faith can be even more personal than sex. Sex can be approached from a physical point of view—what, where, how—body parts, dos and don'ts. If you do X, then Y happens. It's quantifiable, concrete, explainable in its physical formats. Faith is something altogether different. It is not physical; it is spiritual. It is concrete, but its foundations lie in a different realm. *The Message* puts it this way in Hebrews 11:1: "The fundamental fact of existence is that this trust in God, this faith, is the firm foundation under everything that makes life worth living. It's our handle on what we can't see" (MSG). As a Christian parent, you're trying to pass off a handle to your teenager that you know is there, that you desperately want your teen to know is there, and that neither of you can see. This faith baton is tricky. But, like every baton pass-off, it works better if you're actually running the race, you've got a firm grasp on what you want to pass on, you pace yourself to the person you're passing off to, and you get out of the way after it's passed.

Get in the Game

You may not realize it, but you have a great deal of influence over your teenager's faith and belief in God. After all, your children see you every day and watch how your faith intersects and informs your attitudes, your choices, your way of life. Ahhh, but there's the difficulty, isn't it? They see you—every day; they see when you succeed and they see when you fail. They see your sincere efforts, as well as your insincere ones. They see your faults and your imperfections. As a parent, you recognize you exist as a sort of stand-in for God, who is the perfect Parent, and you never are one. You fear that those imperfections are going to present an insurmountable barrier to faith in your child's life. You're afraid you're not going to do enough, know enough, explain enough, and that deficiency is going to translate into a spiritual void in your child's life. You're not just worried that your lack of discipline over doughnuts is going to encourage your child to be fat; you're worried your lack of spiritual discipline is going to doom your child to hell.

This sort of pressure is why, I believe, so many Christian parents leave The God Talk to trained church staff. The stakes are simply too high. Convinced of their incompetence in spiritual matters, some parents don't even enter the race at all; they, in essence, hire out their children's spiritual salvation to paid professionals.

This is not playing the odds. According to a Barna Group report entitled "Evangelism is Most Effective among Kids," only 7 percent of those who came to a personal faith before the age of thirteen did so because of a minister.[1] Parents came out much higher; half of those who made a decision for Christ before the age of thirteen did so because of their parents, with another 20 percent being influenced by a friend or another relative. For ages thirteen to twenty-one, parents and friends ranked similarly at 20 percent each, with another relative cited 16 percent of the time. For this age-group, the influence of ministers dropped to about the same as through media, at 1 percent each. So even though for older teens the percentage for parents dropped from 50 percent to 20 percent, parents were still up there, ranked right alongside the most important teen influencers: their friends. Take heart; you're more important than you know.

As a parent you matter to your teenager's spirituality. You are not required by God, or your teenager, to be perfect in order to be effective. The one perfect person in Scripture is the most notable exception; everyone else is flawed. Your perfection is not a job requirement where God is concerned. Knowledge of your own failings does not disqualify you from presenting your faith. So before you can pick up that baton of faith and pass it along to your teenager, you need to accept that you're in this spiritual race with your teenager and that it's yours to pass. Other people can give you encouragement and motivation and tips on how to run the race more effectively, but you can't pass a baton sitting in the bleachers, no matter how hard you're cheering. You've got to get in the game, the spiritual-formation game, when it comes to your teen.

Getting in the game means giving up the methodology of what I call church as spiritual marinade. This is the concept that, in order for your teenager to emulate your faith, all you need to do is take him or her to church. You cannot expect your kids to develop a vibrant, transferable faith by merely being marinated an hour or ninety minutes a week in church. Now, don't get me wrong here; I believe attending a faith community is very important and will get into the research on that later in the chapter. However, dipping your kids in a weekly spiritual brine is essentially bleacher parenting where faith is concerned. You need to be down on the field, ready to race.

Firm Grasp

So you're in the race; you've accepted your position. The first thing you need to have a firm grasp on is grace. Without it, you'll find it very difficult to have the strength and courage to keep hold of the baton. You also need it because grace is one of the most important concepts your teenager needs you to pass along. Your kids need to see how faith is lived out every day in the lives of flawed, imperfect people; they need to see how grace works in real life. It's one thing for him to read about it in a Bible verse; it's another thing for her to experience it herself through your actions—and it's something even more for him to experience it himself through his own actions.

Firmly grasp on to what you believe. That doesn't mean you have to have an answer for everything; you don't and you won't. Saying "I don't know" is not a spiritual indictment; it's an opportunity for growth and understanding and spiritual maturity. Remember, the definition of faith is that sometimes you're not going to "see" all the answers. Learning to hang on to your faith through times of doubt is part of the baton. Your teen needs to see and understand that doubt in a spiritual answer does not need to equate to a doubt in God.

Doubt doesn't mean there isn't an answer; it just means you don't happen to have it. It's kind of like that analogy of giving a man a fish or teaching a man to fish. When your teen asks spiritual questions and you always have a pat, definitive, this-is-the-way-it-is answer, whether you really feel that way or not, you're giving a fish. But when you start allowing your teen to see how you handle it when you don't have an answer—how you find one or how you learn to live and be patient without one—you're teaching your teen how to fish. Again, these are the higher-level reasoning skills so vital for teens to develop. You can strengthen these skills through Algebra or World History, but you can also strengthen them through Scripture and spiritual inquiry.

And it doesn't mean you have to have your beliefs carved in stone. Spiritual maturity is a process, even for you. Can you imagine how difficult it would be for your teenager to try to grasp hold of faith if you present yourself as an all-knowing, never-wrong, never-changing spiritual behemoth? Your teen is going to look at that baton as a huge, unbearable weight, impossible to pick up and carry. He or she may decide the whole thing is impossible and leave the field altogether.

Firmly grasp what you know, and firmly grasp your faith in a God who is larger than your answers. Allow your teen to grasp the concept of God's infallibility, not your own. He or she already knows you're not perfect so you might as well give up the pretense altogether. You are not required by your teen to be perfect, but you are required to be honest. Remember, teens detest hypocrisy and double standards. Your religion cannot be presented as a "do as I say but not as I do" exercise. Teens will experience you as lukewarm and will, like it says in Revelation 3:16, spew (or spit or vomit) you—and if you're not careful, your religion—out of their mouths. It does no good to try to achieve perfection via pretense. Teens see right through it, and it infuriates them.

Watch Your Pace

If you've ever watched a relay race, you know that the pass-off of the baton is the most precarious part. The first person who is running is, well, running and bearing down on the next person at a fast clip. The second person has to start running in the same direction to get up to speed but has to watch that the pass happens within the specified area. The first person, by necessity, must slow down, and the second person must correspondingly speed up. Only when they are running in sync can the baton be successfully passed. Again, it's tricky, and I've watched many races lost because the baton was dropped during the pass-off.

As a Christian parent, you and your teen need to come into spiritual sync. This means you're going to need to match your pace to your teen's, and that can be a struggle. If you try to go too fast, your teen is going to have a hard time keeping up, and the baton can be dropped. If you're going too slow and your teen is raring to go spiritually, you and your baton can get left in the dust. The only way to set the correct spiritual pace with your teen is to ask questions and then listen.

I spoke earlier about The God Talk, but, really, you should be having spiritual conversations with your kids all the time. Deuteronomy 11:18–20, speaking about God's laws, puts it this way: "Fix these words of mine in your hearts and minds; tie them as symbols on your hands and bind them on your foreheads. Teach them to your children, talking about them when you sit at home and when you walk along the road, when you lie down and when you get up. Write them on the doorframes of your houses and on your gates."

Talking to your kids about spiritual things seems to be easier when they're small. Perhaps they're more in tune with the miraculous and less jaded by approaching adulthood. It can be harder to have those spiritual conversations with your teenagers because they can ask very difficult, very challenging, very confusing spiritual questions. It's quite different explaining to a five-year-old how God made the sky blue than explaining to a fifteen-year-old why a classmate is dying of cancer.

Your teenager, being somewhat fearless, very well may find the most controversial questions to ask you about your faith and about your understanding of God. Answering the questions, as best and as honestly as you can, is keeping pace with your teen. A teenager is all about a quest for truth. Teens' whole world is changing, and they, quite rightly, are looking to find truth to anchor themselves to. As a Christian parent, you want that anchor to be God.

You cannot know where your teen is spiritually if you don't ever talk about it. Keeping pace means keeping the dialogue open. Keeping the dialogue open means answering difficult questions. You can answer difficult questions best if you've thought them over for yourself first. Some older Christians stop seeking answers, preferring to live within a small, defined, and comfortable orthodoxy. This approach doesn't work well with searching teenagers. They want things defined, but they want to do that defining themselves and aren't interested in small or comfortable.

As much as you try to prepare, however, for the spiritual questions your teenagers could ask, you will still come up short. You're still going to honestly answer, "I don't know," to tough questions you haven't thought of before. One way to keep pace with your teenager is to seek the answers to those questions together. This is not you determining the outcome but the two of you journeying toward an understanding together.

As you think about keeping pace with your teenager, be aware that it's not always a situation where you'll need to slow down spiritually; sometimes, you're going to need to speed up. Teenagers on a quest for truth can be extremely vigorous in that pursuit. They can bring all of their high expectations and youthful energy to the task. You may need to spiritually speed up to keep pace with that kind of energy.

Clearing the Lane

The pass-off of a baton requires that the first runner, at the right time, clears the lane so the second runner can run the next leg of the race. You do not ever see the first runner, with a hand still on the baton, trying to continue to run alongside the second runner. In the first place, both runners would be disqualified. In the second, it would be physically cumbersome, and the two could never run as fast or effectively as the one. Yet parents attempt to do this all the time. Because of the eternal stakes involved, some parents are terrified to let go of the faith baton and allow their teenagers to run their own race.

Again, as people, we tend to try to desperately control that which has the capacity to cause us the most pain. For Christian parents, the salvation of their children is top on the list, usually even above their own salvation. Yet they are required to let go of the baton and watch their children run their own race, not knowing the outcome. It can be especially difficult if their teenager, after taking the baton, starts running off in a different direction.

Teenagers have a way of pushing against boundaries and an uncanny ability to know where their parents are most vulnerable. It comes from living in close proximity to you, from listening to you, and from analyzing those boundaries and limitations. Christian parents need to be aware that one of the ways their teenagers may choose to push against those boundaries, to declare independence, may be through how they investigate or demonstrate this personal faith quest. A teenager from a devout Christian home may declare he or she doesn't believe in God and no longer wants to go to church. In an opposite way, a teenager from a home where religion is marginally practiced may declare a deeper devout and passionate belief in God, including becoming involved in more religious activities. A teenager from one denomination or religious background may decide to become involved in a completely different faith community. All of these are ways of testing the waters.

Parents are used to having control over so many aspects of their children's lives and safety. When our children are little, we hold their hands in dangerous situations. As they get bigger, we buy things like knee pads and bike helmets. We put limits on where they can drive, whom they can visit, and what time they need to be home. We impose our boundaries and limitations on them to keep them safe, loosening those boundaries as our children grow and mature and are better able to make good choices for themselves.

There is one thing, though, we don't have control over, and that is the personal faith of our children. We have influence, but we do not have control. Personal faith is, by definition, personal, and every person must stand before God on his or her own. This is a source of genuine anxiety for parents who so longingly want to transfer their own faith to their children.

You cannot transfer your faith to your teenager, but you can let your teenager know your own faith journey, how you came to your faith, and what it has meant up to this point in your life. For some of you, this is extremely difficult because it will reveal struggles and mistakes and circumstances you have been trying to shield your child from. This is because many of us come to faith through fire, through times of extreme personal difficulty. If this is you, it's not necessary to provide your teenager with all the gruesome details, but you can talk about mistakes and regrets you have and how grace, forgiveness, and faith have transformed your life. For other parents, this is difficult because, as long as they can remember, they've had faith; they came to it early and just have hung on through the ups and downs of life.

It's okay to talk about difficult things with your teens. It's okay if you don't have a polished presentation. It's okay if you don't know chapter and verse. Start first with the story of your own faith, how you got there, and how you hold on. This isn't a doctrinal presentation or a Christian apologetics exercise; it's you being open, honest, and real with your teenager. This is the time to open yourself up—the real you, the unsure you, the imperfect you—to your teen. It's an appropriate segue way into your faith in a real, steadfast, perfect, loving God. And the nice thing is, this isn't some sort of evangelistic method. You don't have to memorize anything. It's just your story; it's just you talking about your personal faith.

It is important, in this context, to think about the difference between personal faith and religious practice, especially when it comes to older teenagers. Research conducted for the National Study of Youth and Religion found that as teenagers get older, they start to drift away from things like going to church and attending religious classes. However, teens did not report a corresponding drop in how they felt about their own spirituality. The report conclusions regarding this contradiction stated,

> As we suggested earlier, it may be that adolescents
> place more emphasis on the aspects of religiosity
> that changed the least—belief in God, the
> importance of religion in daily life, and closeness
> to God—when evaluating changes in their
> religiosity as a whole. They may consider religious
> practices to be the least important in their
> life course.... In addition, it could be that as
> adolescents develop and mature, they take more
> ownership over their own beliefs and practices

so that their religiosity feels stronger and more authentic—regardless of the level of belief or behaviors they report.[2]

As teens begin to run their own spiritual race, they may take off in different directions, and some will begin to move away from going to church. As long as they're living with you, however, it is still valuable for them to stay in the churchgoing lane. One study for the National Study of Youth and Religion says:

> [T]he 37 percent of youth with a parent attending worship services at least once a week are significantly more likely than those whose parents do not attend to:

- Have mothers who both praise and are strict with them
- Have mothers who know most things about their close friends' parents and who know who they are with when they are not at home
- Have fathers whom they aspire to be like and of whom they think highly
- Have fathers who are supportive of them and don't tend to abruptly cancel plans with them
- Have fathers who know at least some things about their close friends, about their close friends' parents, about whom they interact

with when not home and about their life
in school

- Eat dinner regularly with their families
- Not run away from home[3]

Did you notice all of the benefits that teenagers experience not
only from going to church themselves but also from going to church
with their parents? Sometimes, the resistance teens display toward
going to church can wear parents down, and one Sunday missed
becomes two. Two Sundays missed become four, and, before very
long at all, a couple of months have gone by, and somehow the sky
hasn't fallen and other things have moved in to fill the Sunday gap.

But a faith community is very important. It provides another
type of family for teens to interact in. It allows and even forces teens
to be in proximity with all ages of people, instead of becoming insu-
lar within their peer group. Going to church socializes teens into the
adult religious world. Not all of them are going to stay there once
they're released into the world on their own, but it still provides a
valuable launching point for their lives:

The 31 percent of all 12th graders who attend
religious services weekly and the 30 percent of
high school seniors for whom religion is very
important are significantly more likely than non-
attenders and the non-religious to

- have positive attitudes toward themselves
- enjoy life as much as anyone

- feel like their lives are useful
- feel hopeful about their futures
- feel satisfied with their lives
- feel like they have something of which to be proud
- feel good to be alive
- feel like life is meaningful
- enjoy being in school[4]

Teenagers are going to start seeking their own paths, and, ultimately, you need to let them go. However, as long as they are in your house, going to church as a family is important and valuable. As long as they are in your house, you are both still in that pass-off zone. This is the time you have to strengthen and fortify their faith, to explain your own, and to be available to help them come to terms with their own spiritual questions and answers.

In this effort, you do not have an ally in society. Again, there is great competition out there for connection with your teenager. One Barna study notes, "While there is still much vibrancy to teen spirituality, it seems to be 'thinning out.' Teenagers view religious involvement partly as a way to maintain their all-important relationships. Yet perhaps technology such as social networking is reconfiguring teens' needs for relationships and continual connectivity, diminishing the role of certain spiritual forms of engagement in their lives. Talking to God may be losing out to Facebook."[5]

There appears to be a sphere of opportunity for spiritual formation that coalesces around adolescence. Teens discover the spiritual voids in their lives and look for ways to fill them. However, the number of teenagers who are seeking traditional religious formats to fill those voids is, as Barna says, "thinning out." Society is more than ready to provide alternatives for connection, a sense of belonging, and a facade of spirituality. It appears the strongest bulwark against this cultural pressure is a strong connection to faith and community in the home. Again, this is your time to make sure your teenager knows how you feel about God and faith, not just about going to church. This baton needs to be passed, and the time is short. Before long, you will need to move out of the way and allow personal faith to grow in your teenager. You cannot predict the outcome, but you can make sure, as long as it depends on you, to provide a rich spiritual soil for that seed to take root.

Drifting Away

Some of you who are reading this book may find yourselves in the position of having gone to church or been involved in a faith community in the past, even the distant past, but this is no longer so. You have, as the term goes, drifted away from your own faith or never really developed one. Perhaps it's time to reexamine that decision and reevaluate the reasons why you continue to remain apart from God or a community of faith.

Faith or religion may not be anything you talk about in your home or with your teenagers, but that doesn't mean they don't think about it. Teenagers are in the midst of asking important life questions such as "Who am I?" and "Why am I here?" These are spiritual quests, regardless of whether they're thought of in a traditional religious sense. I believe that every person, whether self-identified as religious or not, has these spiritual thoughts. It's why my counseling philosophy is called *whole person*—emotional, relational, physical, and spiritual. When you treat the whole person and address each of these aspects, the opportunity for long-term recovery and healing is greatly enhanced.

Your teenager is a whole person—granted, a whole person still in formation—with emotional, relational, physical, and spiritual aspects. The spiritual longings in our lives, I believe, have to do with a sense of belonging and a desire to be a part of something greater than self. Teens, waking up to the fact of their personhood and looking to find a place in the world, desire to make a difference. They want their lives to count for and mean something. Again, all of these are core-level spiritual desires. And teens will have these thoughts and desires even if they never openly discuss them with you.

What do you want your teenager to know about religion, about faith, about God from you? Your teen is watching and evaluating and coming to conclusions based upon your life and how you live it. If you live a life devoid of an acknowledgment of the spiritual, apathetic to or hostile toward faith, this will have a profound effect on your teenager. And those effects, as seen in the studies presented in this chapter, are not positive. Put another way, teenagers who do not attend religious services weekly or for whom religion is not important are significantly less likely to

- have positive attitudes toward themselves
- enjoy life as much as anyone
- feel like their lives are useful
- feel hopeful about their futures

- feel satisfied with their lives
- feel like they have something of which to be proud
- feel good to be alive
- feel like life is meaningful
- enjoy being in school

Many people return to the religion of their roots or to faith in general after they have children. There is something profoundly unsettling to the veneer of control when you've been given a brand-new human being to raise. Because of this, people turn to a faith community for help, for support, for answers and stability. Just because your kids are older now doesn't mean you can't find all those things there waiting for you. It's not too late to return to God. It's not too late to introduce your teenagers to a community of faith. It's not too late to have an open and honest conversation with your teenager about spiritual matters—yours and his or hers.

As parents, we cannot control our teenager's spirituality. We can, however, influence it. The time will come when the baton of spirituality or lack thereof is passed and older teens will be on their own. Life is hard; adulthood is not easy. I want my kids to have seen in my house, in my life, a faith in a personal God, a loving Father, a compassionate Christ, and an empowering Spirit. I'm not interested in hanging on to the baton too long and crowding them out of their lane in life, but I am interested in making sure I pass that faith baton at the appropriate time, matching my pace to theirs, and trusting God to guide them through their own leg of this race called Life.

Bringing It Home

Using the baton analogy within this chapter, I'd like you to answer the following questions:

Are you actively involved with a faith community? If so, why? If not, why not?

Do you feel you've done a good job explaining to your teenager the role faith plays in your life? If so, when was the last time you sat down and had a faith discussion with your teen? Could it be time for another? If you don't think you've adequately discussed your faith with your teen, what would you say to him or her, if you had the chance?

Do you feel you've done a good job modeling the role faith plays in your life? If so, how have you done that? What behaviors or routines have shown your faith? If not, what behaviors or routines have undermined your presentation of faith?

Do you know what your teenager feels about his or her faith? What do you know? How do you know?

Is a discussion on faith a one-way or a two-way exercise? Do you spend most of your time talking to your teenager or listening to your teenager?

Have you ever told your teenager the story of your own faith decision? If not, is that something you could plan to do in the near future, and what would you need to do to prepare?

Have you ever told your teenager about your past failures and mistakes where life and faith are concerned? If so, how do you feel it was received? If not, can you think of a single example that might be relevant to what your teenager is going through right now? Would you be willing to share it? If not, why not? What would need to happen for you to be willing?

If you are a member of a faith community, do you consider it the job of the youth leader to bring your teenager to faith? If so, why? If not, why not?

If you could communicate five spiritual truths you've learned over your life so far, what would they be?

1.
2.
3.
4.
5.

Are you willing to share those with your teenager? If so, when? If not, why not?

Are you willing to ask your teenager to share his or hers? If so, when? If not, why not?

Are you willing to allow your teenager to come to his or her own personal understanding of faith, even if it deviates from yours? In what ways yes and in what ways no?

10

Powerful Parenting

Lord, I'm terrified. I look at my daughter and the direction she appears to be going, and it just seems further and further from You.

Father, when You gave me this precious little boy, I made a promise to raise him for You. Well, the raising is almost over, and I'm afraid I've messed up my promise.

Lord, I've done everything I could to pass on my beliefs, and I'm not sure it's enough because she seems to have more questions now than ever.

Father, if there was a way to secure his salvation, I'd do it. I'd pay whatever price was necessary.

God, I understand You now, more than ever.

In some ways, raising kids is an immersion into the divine. I don't know about you, but the first thought that comes to my mind when I see pictures of a new little human being formed is *miraculous.* The second thought that comes to mind is Psalm 139:13: "For you created my inmost being; you knit me together in my mother's womb." To experience life and birth is to experience the miraculous, the divine.

And once you know that this child you've been given is part of the divine, there comes a sense of immense responsibility. You haven't been given a thing, an object, to take care of or money to steward; you've been given a human being, a soul, to love and cherish and nurture. As Psalm 139 also says, "Such knowledge is too wonderful for me, too lofty for me to attain" (v. 6).

But when that child is new and small and malleable, the responsibility seems easier. After all, you've got some time to work into this parenting thing, this "raising them up in the Lord" thing. By the time that child hits adolescence, as a parent, you realize how quickly you're running out of time.

The book of Ecclesiastes says, "There is a time for everything, and a season for every activity under heaven" (3:1). You are in the season of adolescent parenting; it's a season that's here for only a short amount of time, with an expiration date. So why is it that just when you figure out the clock is winding down on your parenting years and time is short, it seems like it's harder than ever to pass your faith on to your teenager? As your teen moves from dependence on you to independence, you want to direct him or her to voluntarily choose both independence from you and dependence on God. And you want all this, preferably, before age eighteen so you can have just a small vision of it to rejoice over and hang on to when your teen is out of the house. Talk about pressure.

As I said earlier, parents in general have a lot to worry about where their kids are concerned. Christian parents have an added spiritual dimension of eternal proportions. The only way, I think, to be able to manage this pressure is to remember back to that feeling you had at your teen's birth—with your recognition of the miraculous and the divine. Be honest; you knew when you held that baby for the first time that you were out of your league. You still are. Your child's life, including salvation, has always been in God's hands; it was just easier to see it back then when your son or daughter was small and cuddly, without all that adolescent attitude and teenage hormones. That precious little soul is still in there, still incubating, still being woven together by God just as surely as sinew and muscle and bone.

Raising Up a Child

One of the most famous biblical passages on parenting has been presented as a good-news-bad-news type of pronouncement: "Train up a child in the way he should go: and when he is old, he will not depart from it" (Prov. 22:6 KJV). It's good news because there is a concreteness to it, an implied promise—if A, then B. If you do it right, she's in. Which leads to the bad news part: If you do it wrong, he's out. And every Christian parent, at some point, worries and stresses over doing it wrong.

Perhaps we've focused on the wrong things where this verse is concerned. We've focused on our part of this whole training process when we should be focusing instead on God's. Instead of this verse serving as a personal indictment of my failures and shortcomings as a parent, I choose to see the promises this way:

God's truth is powerful. When Scripture talks about "train up a child," I don't think it's talking about merely a set of rules to adhere to. Rather, I believe it's talking about presenting the truth about God as a foundation for living. God's truth is a powerful beacon, pointing people in the way they should go in life. This truth is so powerful, its affects are lifelong and life changing.

God's truth endures. There will come a time in everyone's life when adolescence ends and maturity begins to surface. I've experienced it in my own life; it's that moment when you realize how truly remarkable and smart your parents are. You start having those "aha" moments about things they said or concepts they kept drilling into your head. God's truth is like your parents' truth on steroids. It has effect, as this beautiful passage from Isaiah illustrates:

> As the rain and the snow
>   come down from heaven,
> and do not return to it
>   without watering the earth
> and making it bud and flourish,
>   so that it yields seed for the sower and bread for the
>   eater,
> so is my word that goes out from my mouth:
>   It will not return to me empty,
> but will accomplish what I desire
>   and achieve the purpose for which I sent it.
>   (55:10–11)

The book of Hebrews uses a different analogy for the power of God's truth: "For the word of God is living and active. Sharper than any double-edged sword, it penetrates even to dividing soul and spirit, joints and marrow; it judges the thoughts and attitudes of the heart" (4:12).

As a parent, when you have introduced and presented God's truth to your child, to your teenager, it will have an effect. The power belongs to God, not to you. This is why it is so important that teenagers read God's Word and develop their own relationship with Him, even if it looks different from their parents'. Do you trust God's Word and truth to be powerful enough to speak into your teen's life without you there to interpret? Do you trust God's Word and truth to be powerful enough to speak into your teen's life even though it came through you?

Messing Up the Message

Are you raising a teenager? Are you a human being? If you answered yes to both those questions, you're going to mess up. You are not perfect as a person; therefore, you will not be perfect as a parent, no matter how many parenting books you read. So jettison perfection as a parental requirement. It's not your job to do everything perfectly in order for your teenager to see God. You are not the only reflection of God your teenager has available. Romans 1:20 says that nature itself is a God-created canvas to highlight His "invisible qualities—his eternal power and divine nature." God is making sure your teenager knows and sees Him even if He has to go through you to do it.

When you earnestly desire for your teenager to know and see God, you join with God's purpose and plans. This desire isn't original to you. Remember the Isaiah passage you just read? God has a desire to accomplish and a purpose to what He does. Part of what He desires and purposes is a relationship with your teenager: "The Lord is not slow in keeping his promise, as some understand slowness. He is patient with you, not wanting anyone to perish, but everyone to come to repentance" (2 Peter 3:9). The "anyone" includes your teenager, and He is willing to be patient. Are you?

God has also factored in your "messiness" where His message is concerned. And believe me, this messiness didn't start with you. People have been messing up God's message since, well, the beginning, and God has factored this in: "For God, who said, 'Let light shine out of darkness,' made his light shine in our hearts to give us the light of the knowledge of the glory of God in the face of Christ. But we have this treasure in jars of clay to show that this all-surpassing power is from God and not from us" (2 Cor. 4:6–7). Did you catch where all this started, as far as God is concerned? When He said, "Let light shine out of darkness"—that's Genesis 1. Your messiness in delivering His message has been factored in since the beginning. The power to give the message is God's power, taking you into account. As a parent, it's not all up to you.

God doesn't expect you to be perfect as a parent, but He does instruct you to be honest and transparent as a parent. He expects you to pass along what you know and have learned about Him to your children, and not just when they are small. You are not your teenager's only instructor in spiritual things, but you are an important one, as you read earlier. Your life becomes the lesson book, and everyday things become conduits into the divine: "Teach them to your children, talking about them when you sit at home and when you walk along the road, when you lie down and when you get up" (Deut. 11:19). Your life should be a constant spiritual conversation with your teenager, not periodic religious lectures.

It's not just about you instructing your teen in spiritual things; you also have a responsibility to remain spiritually "sharp" yourself. Earlier in Deuteronomy there is this admonition: "Only be careful, and watch yourselves closely so that you do not forget the things your eyes have seen or let them slip from your heart as long as you live. Teach them to your children and to their children after them" (4:9). Your parental responsibility is to teach, to walk about, to show, and to explain who God is to you and what He's done in your life. This is your testimony, messy though it is, and it's what your teenager needs to hear, more than merely memorizing a list of dos and don'ts.

You have more power in your corner than you realize. Actually, all that power isn't in your corner as much as you are able to move to the corner with all that power. Salvation and faith are really in God's corner. God, who knows your teenager, is actively working to bring him or her to Himself. You have a part to play, but you are not in control. You have power to present, to persuade, to proclaim the good news to your teenager. What you do not have is the power to force, coerce, manipulate, or maneuver your teenager into an authentic faith in God. Such efforts honor and benefit no one.

The Power of Trust

How much do you trust God? You say you do; you tell your teenager you do. But how much do you really trust Him? I've found parents often place far greater trust in the bad things that can happen to their kids than the good things. It's as if evil and disaster and trouble are more reliable than God when it comes to their kids. So they make sure to keep pessimism or pragmatism close but somehow misplace optimism. How you respond to calamities—even small ones—reveals where you've placed your trust and what "ism" you've partnered with where your teenager is concerned.

We've already talked about the tendency teenagers have toward black-and-white thinking. As a parent, I caution you against this same kind of thinking about your teenager, especially about the mistakes your teenager will inevitably make. Some parents have such a narrowly defined vision of what success looks like for their teenager, including spiritual success, they develop a one-strike-and-you're-out mentality. One difference, one deviation from the rigidly defined parameters, and the teen is "out." This is putting ultimate trust in a mistake to ruin a life over God's power to redeem it.

It is also putting trust in the status quo of your teenager being and acting always like an adolescent. It's pupa vision instead of butterfly vision. It can seem like the teen years drag on forever, but they really don't. It can seem like your teen is just averse to learning or growing or maturing, but that isn't so for most kids. You want to trust in God's ability to overcome rather than in your or your kid's power to screw things up, but it's hard when you're in the midst of dealing with your own messiness as well as your teenager's. In order to gain more trust, maybe what you need is a different perspective.

The Power of Perspective

I'll never forget when I switched from a short, little compact car to a large SUV. This vehicular swap is part of parenting, I think, because kids require stuff and stuff requires space, and those larger SUVs have space to haul all that stuff and all those friends. After spending time so close to the road in that little subcompact, it was a revelation to climb up into the cab of the SUV, to be up just an additional couple of feet. Same road, but things just looked different; it was a different perspective.

Maybe, in order to improve your trust as a parent, you need to gain a different perspective—same road, same life, same teenager, just a little different viewpoint. Instead of perennially viewing your teenager as a whiny, annoying, demanding, ungrateful adolescent, why not ask God to begin to show you what your teenager looks like from His perspective? He's up a little higher than you are and has a pretty good grasp on the long view. Why not ask God to reveal to you a bit of what He sees, as a way for you to have hope and to navigate this difficult teenager phase?

Think about your own life and how much you've changed as an adult. And don't just think about the negative ways! Consider how you've grown and matured, how you've come to understand life and priorities better because of age and experience. The seeds for those changes are being watered and nurtured in your teenager right now. You're in the midst of the planting season, and, frankly, you're a little tired of pulling rocks out of the soil and weeds out of the ground and waiting for the rain to fall. Ask God to give you a glimpse into what the harvest is going to be like for your teenager.

Notice I didn't say to ask God to give you a glimpse of the harvest you envision but rather a glimpse of what the harvest is actually going to be like. When you're dealing with perspective, the last thing you want to get in the way is a big barrier of personal preferences and expectations. God's view isn't jaded by yours; He sees what is real and true.

It's also possible that those personality traits in your teenager that drive you the most nuts are the very ones God is honing for His purposes later on. Tenacity as an adult is often experienced as stubbornness in childhood. Boldness later in life can come across as impertinence in a kid. As you're asking God to give you some perspective, you might consider asking Him to show you how He can use the things about your teenager that bug you the most.

The Power of Forgiveness

Have you ever had a problem with your car where you could actually hear the gears grinding against each other? When things are supposed to be working together and end up out of alignment, it results in a lot of grinding and scraping; it's abrasive—kind of like adolescence. This age isn't just *teens in transition;* it's *teens as transmission.* You and your teen are going along down the road of life together, but often you're in different gears and end up scraping and grating against each other. It can be nails-on-a-chalkboard-times-ten irritating.

It is during this time that every scrape and grate and grind, if left untreated, can fester and erode the quality of your relationship. He lashes out and you yell back. She drops the ball and you fling it in her face. He walks out the door and you slam it behind him. She retreats into herself and you leave her there.

Why is it that as we age we lose so much flexibility? I don't just mean physical flexibility; I mean emotional flexibility. The older we get, the harder it becomes to bend and stretch and forgive. In order to get through this time of adolescence, teens need to hang on to their ability to forgive, and adults need to rediscover it. Otherwise both are left in the black-and-white world of one-strike-and-you're-out.

God's forgiveness parameters are not so narrowly defined; He gives us far more than one chance or even three strikes. The apostle Peter once asked Jesus how many times he was required to forgive someone and suggested seven times. Doesn't seven times seem like a lot to you? Can you imagine forgiving someone for cheating you seven times or stealing your car seven times? Jesus replied not seven but seventy-seven (Matt. 18:21–23). Seventy-seven or, in the King James Version, seventy *times* seven, are you kidding? How could you be expected to forgive somebody that many times? Is that reasonable? What about treating you unfairly that many times or hurting your feelings or breaking your heart or letting you down? Now we're into the realm of family because we rarely let other people into our lives far enough to do that kind of damage and have that many chances to hurt us.

The grinding and scraping and grating of adolescence require the healing balm of forgiveness in order to regain relational alignment. And you're going to need to go first. It is imperative for you to model asking for, receiving, and giving forgiveness. I'm not sure, from a relational point of view, if there is anything more important for you to teach your teenager as an adult skill. Because we live messy lives and we want to live those lives together with other people, forgiveness is a must.

How do you ask for forgiveness? Do you? When you clearly mess up, do you admit it? Do you try to pretend it didn't happen by not saying anything? Do you try to even the scales by bringing up other issues? Do you try to buy forgiveness as a way to avoid asking for it? These are the sorts of lessons you're teaching your children about forgiveness as you sit at home, as you walk along the road, as you lie down, and as you get up. They may not be the lessons you want to teach, but they're the ones that are speaking out loud and clear to your teenager.

As an adult, I admit I have a problem admitting when I'm wrong. The more wrong I am, the more I've messed up, the harder it is to admit. It's easier for me to admit I ate the last cookie without throwing out the bag than it is to admit when I've snapped at my wife or kids. I just don't want to admit when I've screwed up something so vital, something I know and teach and try to help other people do. I don't want to admit that I've failed at something I spend a great deal of time placing importance in. It's frustrating and very human.

What about you? Do you sometimes just walk away after you've hurt someone, desperately deciding the other person will just have to let it slide and not bring it up? Do you try to minimize how bad it was by revising what you meant or said in your mind? Do you create a mental comparison list—with column A being the way you messed up this one time and column B being all the ways through time immemorial that the other person has? Is it easier for you to say, "I'm sorry," with a thing instead of with words? Is it easier for you to say, "I'm sorry," than "Can you forgive me?"

If you haven't been demonstrating to your teenager the positive power of forgiveness, you've been dropping the ball on one of the most fundamental spiritual concepts (with the first being love). If your child didn't figure it out before hitting puberty, he or she is probably very clued in now about your shortcomings as a person and as a parent. They are, after all, on constant display. By this behavior you have demonstrated the need for forgiveness but not how to accomplish it. That's only part of the lesson.

By asking for someone's forgiveness, you transfer power. That's why I think it's easier to say, "I'm sorry," than it is to ask, "Can you forgive me?" Don't get me wrong—admitting your responsibility and expressing remorse are good, but they only go partway. It is you, still in control, establishing how you feel about what happened. When you ask, "Can you forgive me?" you have to listen and wait for the answer, which could be "not now" or even "no."

When dealing with teens, it's important for you to ask the question. They need to understand the power they have over a hurtful situation. They need to learn that what they think about what's happened to them matters. They need to learn they have the last say.

Having the last say gives the hurt person back the control he or she lost through the injury.

It is tempting to try to make excuses, to mitigate the injury when you've hurt another person, but it is so important that you avoid this temptation. Sometimes, your words or behaviors hurt someone else without conscious intent. It's still important to understand the other perspective and express remorse over the unintended pain.

What about the other way around? What about when your teenager really hurts you? How do you react? Do you talk about what the injury feels like and what it means to you? Do you grant forgiveness without being asked for it? With teenagers, I think it's good to explain how their actions affect you. These are the consequences they find so difficult at this age to reconcile with actions. I don't think you have to purge yourself of all emotion when you talk about them, but I do think you need to be careful not to approach your teenager in anger, rage, or condemnation. You don't want to shout so loudly your teen can't hear what you're saying.

In the best sense, forgiveness should be a two-way conversation. It should be you explaining how you feel and your teenager responding and asking questions and explaining back the whys. If your teenager really understands the hurt he or she has caused, hopefully there will be an expression of remorse and a request for forgiveness. Just be aware it might not happen all at once. Teenagers need more processing time. And I don't think it's necessary right away to express your willingness to forgive. The very fact you've had the conversation and were willing to be open and honest about what happened and how you feel about it indicates your forgiveness. Sometimes, I think forgiveness is best understood when it's been specifically asked for by your teenager instead of granted as a blanket pardon. If asking for forgiveness specifically is good for you, it's also good for your teenager.

So be patient. That's kind of been a theme all through this book. They're young; they're not done yet. They still have growing and maturing to do. You should be able to empathize because you were a teenager once yourself and you haven't exactly completed the growing and maturing portion of the life test either.

The Power of Prayer

While you wait for all of this growing and maturing to take place, I recommend you spend part of that time in prayer. If this stage in life were easy, you wouldn't have picked up this book in the first place. It's not—not for you, not for your teen. Both of you need divine guidance and direction to navigate these waters.

Prayer reminds you that you're not in this alone. When you're stressed out because it's up to you to find the lost science paper or the perfect pair of shoes or fill out the permission slip or get to practice on time, parenting can seem like a solitary proposition. It's not. Even if you are a single parent, you're not in it by yourself. You have help and resources beyond yourself to assist you as you handle your role as parent.

Prayer encourages you to release the illusion of control. There is something about being on your knees, metaphorically or physically, that puts things into proper perspective. We are not in control of so much of what life sends our way. Our control lies within our response. When our response is to turn to God, we join ourselves to God's immense power. It's much easier for me to relinquish my own control when I know the power over my situation rests with God.

Prayer helps clarify your thoughts. There is something about putting your thoughts into words that brings them into focus. Prayer, as a conversation, can do the same thing. I guarantee there are times you won't know what to pray for your teenager. You'll be so frustrated or angry or frightened, words won't come easily. Don't let this deter you. Pray anyway; allow the Spirit to help define your thoughts. Because I'm a writer, I tend to think in words. Other people think through music or pictures or patterns. Prayer is an individual communication between you and God; and God, knowing you best, will use whatever means are most effective to help facilitate your conversation.

Prayer allows you to listen to God. Prayer is really a two-way conversation. It is us pouring out our hearts and our thoughts to God, but it is also His Spirit speaking to us. Sometimes, I am so insistent on telling God what I think, I don't take time to stop long enough to listen to what He thinks. I get impatient and want a response *right now!* But the best, most effective prayer is when I wait on God, patient but expectant, to hear what He has to say to me about what I've just prayed. As you pray for your teenager, adopt the same attitude; don't get up too soon.

Prayer gives you hope. Sharing a concern with God creates a partnership. As you come face-to-face with your own shortcomings and failings as a parent, it can be overwhelming. But when you are partnered in your parenting with God, there is always hope, even in the midst of struggles. I love Romans 5:3–5, which talks about the power of hope in our lives. It says that through hope we can weather the troubles we face because those struggles produce perseverance, which results in an increase in our "proven character" (NASB).

Fortified in character, we have the strength to cling even more tightly to hope, which "does not disappoint." As the parent of a teenager, you need to cling tightly to hope to weather this time.

Trust in God, even when you've lost trust in yourself and in your teen.

Forget about perfection, either for yourself or for your teenager. It's not going to happen anyway so you might as well just admit it and move on. Go for growth, instead—and trust God to use even the bad things that happen to produce that growth (Rom. 8:28).

Learn to see your teenager through God's eyes. Take off your expectation spectacles and learn to accept the truth. Ignorance may be bliss, but you need to parent with both eyes open, alert to what's ahead because your teenager won't always be able to see what's coming. Scripture is pretty clear about what happens when the blind lead the blind (Luke 6:39). Teenager parenting is a heads-up proposition.

Love your teenager. So much of what's happening in his or her life is changing; allow your love, acceptance, and support for who your teen is (not necessarily always for what he or she does) to be the anchor. You want to be your teenager's anchor; teens can tie themselves to so many other things.

Look for ways to enjoy this time of life. I know that seems counterintuitive after all this book's been about, but don't allow the negative to obscure the positives. Watch for the positives, and hang on to them for dear life. Hold them as the precious gifts they are, and guard your heart with them.

Allow your teenager to give you joy today. That's all you've been given, really—just today. Tomorrow is something you've merely penciled in. Don't spend so much time looking and waiting for the good stuff to come that you overlook and downplay the good that's right in front of you. If you have to, scratch around to find it. Remember, treasures have a way of being covered in dirt, but they're worth it.

Bringing It Home

Scripture says that children are a gift and a blessing from God (Ps. 127:4–5). That part may have gotten overlooked lately in your house, so perhaps now would be a good time to be reminded. Name three ways God has blessed you through your teenager:

1.
2.
3.

When it comes to your child, it can be easy to succumb to fear about his or her future. It can be easier to trust in calamity than in God, even though, as a Christian, you do trust in God. In the book of Mark (9:14–29), there is a story about a man who brings his son to the disciples to be healed. The disciples, however, are unable to do it. When Jesus arrives, the man explains the situation and the disciples' failure and says, "If you can do anything, take pity on us and help us." I think this is often how we pray, as parents, with an "if you can" attitude because we don't really think God is more powerful than the situation. Jesus calls the man out for using "if" and tells him, "Everything is possible for him who believes." The man quickly proclaims that he does believe but then asks Jesus, "Help me overcome my unbelief!"

I would like you to list three things you believe God can do regarding your teen:

1.
2.
3.

Now, I'd like you to put into words the source of your unbelief. Where do you doubt that God is powerful enough to act in your teenager's life? Where is the source of your unbelief?

Going forward, what are the truths you want your teenager to know and understand about God, and how are you going to model those in your own life? For each truth, complete the following two statements:

I Want My Teen to Know:
I Will Model It in This Way:

As you read over the section in the chapter on forgiveness, what did you learn about yourself and the ways you deal with forgiveness?

The next time you hurt your teenager, how are you going to respond differently?

The next time your teenager hurts you, how are you going to respond differently?

As a way to bring some perspective to this last Bringing It Home section, I encourage you to go back and read through each Bringing It Home section again. Refresh your memory about what you've learned and the insights you've determined to carry with you going forward.

It is important for you to spend time in prayer for your teenager and for yourself as a parent of a teenager. As often as you pray for your teenager, I'd like you to include the following, based on the ACTS prayer method (Adoration, Confession, Thanksgiving, Supplication):

A—Praise God for being the perfect Parent, able to give you wisdom, guidance, and direction in raising your teen.

C—Confess your own shortcomings as a parent, and acknowledge your need for His help in your life.

T—Thank God for the life of your teenager today even with the struggles you're facing.

S—Ask God to guide you and your teen to a greater understanding of who He is, more awareness of His presence in your lives, and a stronger bond to Him and to each other.

The rest is up to you, your teen, and God, with an emphasis on the God part.

Notes

Chapter 3: Emotional Roller Coasters Aren't Very Fun

1. "The Teenage Brain: A Work in Progress," National Institute of Mental Health, NIMH Publication 1 4929, http://www.nimh.nih.gov/health/publications/teenage-brain-a-work-in-progress-fact-sheet/index.shtml.

2. Ibid.

3. Jay N. Giedd et al., "Puberty-Related Influences on Brain Development," *Molecular and Cellular Endocrinology* 254–55 (2006): 154–162, http://intramural.nimh.nih.gov/chp/articles/giedd-2006-mce.pdf.

4. "Adolescent Brains Show Lower Activity in Areas That Control Risky Choices," National Institute of Mental Health, March 15, 2007, http://www.nimh.nih.gov/science-news/2007/adolescent-brains-show-lower-activity-in-areas-that-control-risky-choices.shtml.

5. Olivier J. Y. Monneuse, "Attitudes about Injury among High School Students," *Journal of American College of Surgeons* 207.2 (August 2008): 179–84, http://www.journalacs.org/article/S1072-7515(08)00075-6/abstract.

6. "Sense of Invincibility Among Teens' Attitudes to Trauma-Related Injury, Especially Those Due to Motor Vehicle Crashes," *Medical News Today,* August 16, 2008, http://www.medicalnewstoday.com/articles/118346.php.

7. Ibid.

Chapter 4: Shaky Connections

1. Reinhold Niebuhr, "The Serenity Prayer," public domain.

2. Amanda Lenhart et al., "Teens and Mobile Phones," Pew Internet, April 20, 2010, http://pewinternet.org/Reports/2010/Teens-and-Mobile-Phones.aspx.

3. Ibid.

4. Matt Richtel, "E-mail Gets an Instant Makeover," *New York Times,* December 20, 2010, http://www.nytimes.com/2010/12/21/technology/21email.html?_r=1&hp.

5. Lenhart et al., "Teens and Mobile Phones."

Chapter 5: This Is Your Body on Adolescence

1. Rhoskel K. Lenroot et al., "Sexual Dimorphism of Brain Developmental Trajectories during Childhood and Adolescence," *NeuroImage* 36 (2007): 1065–73.

2. William D. S. Killgore and Deborah A. Yurgelun-Todd, "Sex-Related Developmental Differences in the Lateralized Activation of the Prefrontal Cortex and Amygdala during Perception of Facial Affect," *Perceptual and Motor Skills* 99 (2004): 371–91.

3. J. C. Abma, G. M. Martinez, and C. E. Copen, "Teenagers in the United States: Sexual Activity, Contraceptive Use, and Childbearing, National Survey of Family Growth 2006–2008," National Center for Health Statistics, *Vital Health and Statistics* 23.30 (2010): 1.

Chapter 6: When There's More Along for the Ride

1. "Cigarette Use Among High School Students," Centers for Disease Control and Prevention, *Morbidity and Mortality Weekly Report* 59.26 (July 9, 2010): 1, http://www.cdc.gov/mmwr/preview/mmwrhtml/mm5926a1.htm?s_cid=mm5926a1_w.

2. "Tobacco Addiction," NIDA for Teens, http://teens.drugabuse.gov/facts/facts_nicotine1.php.

3. "Teen Smoking: 10 Ways to Help Teens Stay Smoke-Free," Mayo Foundation for Medical Education and Research, June 17, 2009, http://www.mayoclinic.com/health/teen-smoking/HQ00139.

4. "Shoplifting Statistics," National Association for Shoplifting Prevention, 2006, http://www.shopliftingprevention.org/WhatNASPOffers/NRC/PublicEducStats.htm.

5. Ibid.

6. Ibid.

7. Ibid.

8. "Anxiety Disorders," National Institute for Mental Health, NIMH Publication 9 3879 (2009): 4.

9. "Alcohol & Drug Use," Centers for Disease Control and Prevention, August 8, 2008, http://www.cdc.gov/HealthyYouth/alcoholdrug/index.htm.

10. Office of the Surgeon General, "The Surgeon General's Call to Action to Prevent and Reduce Underage Drinking," U.S. Department of Health and Human Services, 2007.

11. "Alcohol & Drug Use," Centers for Disease Control and Prevention.

Chapter 8: When It's Time to Get Help

1. "Antidepressent Use in Children, Adolescents, and Adults," U.S. Food and Drug Administration, 2007, http://www.fda.gov/cder/drug/antidepressants/default.htm.

2. Ibid.

Chapter 9: Crisis of Belief

1. "Evangelism Is Most Effective among Kids," The Barna Group, *Barna Update,* October 11, 2004, http://www.barna.org/barna-update/article/5-barna-update/0196-evangelism-is-most-effective-among-kids.

2. Melinda Denton, Lisa Pearce, and Christian Smith, "Religion and Spirituality on the Path through Adolescence," *A Research Report of the National Study of Youth and Religion* 8 (2008): 31–32, http://www.youthandreligion.org/sites/youthandreligion.org/files/imported/publications/docs/w2_pub_report_final.pdf.

3. Christian Smith and Phillip Kim, "Family Religious Involvement and the Quality of Family Relationships for Early Adolescents," *A Research Report of the National Study of Youth and Religion* 4 (2003): 6, http://www.youthandreligion.org/sites/youthandreligion.org/files/imported/publications/docs/family-report.pdf.

4. Christian Smith and Robert Faris, "Religion and Life Attitudes and Self-Images of American Adolescents," *A Research Report of the National Study of Youth and Religion* 2 (2002): 7, http://www.youthandreligion.org/sites/youthandreligion.org/files/imported/ publications/docs/Attitudes.pdf.

5. "How Teenagers' Faith Practices Are Changing," The Barna Group, July 12, 2010, http://www.barna.org/teens-next-gen-articles/403-how-teenagers-faith-practices-are-changing?q=teenagers+teens.

Books by Gregory L. Jantz, PhD

The Body God Designed. Lake Mary, FL: Strang, 2008.

Every Woman's Guide to Managing Your Anger. Grand Rapids, MI: Revell, 2009.

Gotta Have It! Freedom from Wanting Everything Right Here, Right Now. Colorado Springs: David C Cook, 2010.

Happy for the Rest of Your Life. Lake Mary, FL: Strang, 2009.

Healing the Scars of Emotional Abuse. Grand Rapids, MI: Revell, 1995, 2009.

Healthy Habits, Happy Kids. Grand Rapids, MI: Revell, 2006.

Hope, Help, and Healing for Eating Disorders. Colorado Springs: Waterbrook, 1995, 2010.

How to De-Stress Your Life. Spire, 2008.

Losing Weight Permanently. Spire, 2004.

The Molding of a Champion. Green Forest, AR: New Leaf Press, 2006.

Moving beyond Depression: A Whole Person Approach to Healing. Colorado Springs: Waterbrook, 2003.

Overcoming Anxiety, Worry and Fear: Practical Ways to Find Peace. Grand Rapids, MI: Revell, 2011.

Total Temple Makeover. West Monroe, LA: Howard, 2005.

Thin over 40. New York: Penguin, 2004.

Additional Resources

The following are several books I've found useful in working with teens and parents. They are presented as suggestions for you to consider.

Berry, Richard L. *Angry Kids: Understanding and Managing the Emotions That Control Them*. Grand Rapids, MI: Revell, 2001.

Brizendine, Louann. *The Female Brain*. New York: Broadway Books, 2006.

Chapman, Gary. *The Five Love Languages of Teenagers*. Chicago: Northfield, 2010.

Cobain, Bev. *When Nothing Matters Anymore: A Survival Guide for Depressed Teens*. Minneapolis: Free Spirit, 1998.

Copeland, Mary Ellen, and Stuart Copans. *Recovering from Depression: A Workbook for Teens* (Revised Edition). Baltimore: Paul H. Brookes, 2002.

Hart, Arch, and Catherine Hart Weber. *Is Your Teen Stressed or Depressed? A Practical and Inspirational Guide for Parents of Hurting Teenagers*. Nashville: Thomas Nelson, 2005.

Larson, Susie. *Growing Grateful Kids: Teaching Them to Appreciate an Extraordinary God in Ordinary Places*. Chicago: Moody, 2010.

Mondimore, Francis Mark. *Adolescent Depression: A Guide for Parents*. Baltimore: The Johns Hopkins University Press, 2002.

Oster, Gerald, and Sarah S. Montgomery. *Helping Your Depressed Teenager: A Guide for Parents and Caregivers*. New York: John Wiley & Sons, 1995.

VanVonderen, Jeff. *Families Where Grace Is in Place: Getting Free from the Burden of Pressuring, Controlling, and Manipulating Your Spouse and Children*. Minneapolis: Bethany, 1992, 2010.